Z 33 34844 3

LONDON BOROUGH OF GREENWICH

GREENWICH LIBRARIES

RESERVE STOCK (P)

LIB.116

D0312036

GREENWICH LIBRARIES

3 8028 00853487 4

Master
BRIDGE

Master
BRIDGE

Nicola Gardener

MACMILLAN LONDON

in association with
Channel Four Television Company Limited

SBN 1	2	3
333	34844	3, 2

EDITION DATE	1983.

CLASS NO.	795 4158

| INVOICE Jm | 21·12·83 | £5·95 |

Copyright © Nicola Gardener 1983

All rights reserved. No part of this publication
may be reproduced or transmitted, in any form
or by any means, without permission.

ISBN 0 333 34844 3

First published 1983 by
Macmillan London Limited
London and Basingstoke

Associated companies in Auckland, Dallas,
Delhi, Dublin, Hong Kong, Johannesburg, Lagos,
Manzini, Melbourne, Nairobi,
New York, Singapore, Tokyo, Washington
and Zaria

The television series *Master Bridge*
has been produced for Channel 4
by Brook Productions

Photography by Robert Haas

Filmset in Palatino by Filmtype Services Ltd,
Scarborough, North Yorkshire
Printed in Hong Kong

Contents

Introduction

This book is an account of a remarkable individual contract bridge tournament featuring six of the best British players: the indomitable Mrs Rixi Markus and Mrs Jane Priday, both former World Champions, Jeremy Flint, Martin Hoffman, Irving Rose and Robert Sheehan, supplemented by Zia Mahmood, the champion from Pakistan, and Omar Sharif, the Egyptian film star, who now lives in France.

The conditions of play involved each participant partnering each other participant for four deals, using a form of duplicate scoring to minimize the effect of luck. The event took place on one day in July 1982 in London, and was recorded for first showing on the British Channel 4. Participants were in the studio from 09.00 hours and they played seven sets of four boards. This meant that each player played at least four boards at a time and, with the exception of the pivot Rixi Markus, occasionally eight boards consecutively, sometimes with a short break of only fifteen minutes. Forty minutes were allowed for each playing session of four boards but usually, for technical reasons, this time was exceeded. The strain of playing for so long a time under arc lights and in such unfamiliar conditions obviously affected the performance of all the players to differing extents; it was a test of stamina which ran for nearly seventeen hours. In the circumstances it is perhaps surprising that so many of the difficult plays and defences were found. Unfortunately in this event unfamiliar partnerships were formed at very short notice; consequently the final contracts attained were not always the best. This meant that the prepared problems in each hand did not necessarily arise, but others did. Nevertheless the standard of bridge was reasonable and the objective, to present on television experts playing live in competition, was successfully achieved.

Because of the need to have interesting hands for the viewing public it was decided to have them prepared in advance. This was one of my tasks but I did have the valuable assistance of Bob Rowlands and Derek Rimington, which I gratefully acknowledge.

Set hands also gave me a considerable advantage in writing this book, to what would otherwise have been an impossible timescale. I was able to describe the salient points of each hand, giving the likely bidding and probable initial lead. All of this was undertaken before the actual individual contest took place. Readers may therefore have a bonus. Not only do they see my preview and recommended line of play or defence but they may read about how expert players try to change the course of destiny. Not all contracts turn out to be the same as I forecast, even those which are similar undergo different treatment as acknowledged masters of their craft meet in head-to-head combat. Thrust and counter thrust is made, and hitherto undiscovered facets of famous hands see the light of day. It should all make for the enhanced enjoyment of readers and viewers.

The aim of this book is the same as that of the television programme – to make expert technique understandable to the average player. To this end each prepared hand contains a 'tip' in the bidding, play or defence which is given as a footnote. The purpose of setting it out in this fashion is so that the reader can try to solve the play problem without the aid of the tip.

How Duplicate Bridge Is Played

Duplicate or tournament bridge differs from rubber bridge in that hands are replayed. This is made possible by using numbered boards which state clearly the dealer and the vulnerability. The four players in Room 1 remove their thirteen cards from a pocket in the board and bid the cards as if they had been dealt at the table. When the auction is over play proceeds as in rubber bridge, but with one vital difference – the cards are not mixed together. Instead they remain in front of each player face down, with the length of each card pointing in the direction of the side which took the trick. At the end of the play period the score, according to the stated vulnerability, is agreed and then each hand is returned to its appropriate slot in the board. Scoring is similar to that used in rubber bridge except that honours do not count. A successful part score contract earns an additional bonus of 50 points, and a game 300 or 500 respectively, depending on whether not vulnerable or vulnerable. Slam bonuses and penalty points are the same as in rubber bridge.

3

Individual Contest

In this tournament, after each set of four boards had been played they were replayed by the other four participants. There are thus two results for each board, hence the term duplicate bridge. By adding the score achieved by the North–South pair in Room 1 to that of the East–West pair in Room 2, a net score plus or minus is obtained. This is the score that all four players receive. In effect on any one board there are four players playing as a team against the other four players. For each set of four boards, therefore, the composition of the two teams remains unchanged. It is only when partnerships are altered after each set that a player will also have different team members in the other room.

The winner of the tournament is the player who achieves the highest score over the twenty-eight boards with seven different partners and seven different pairs of team mates in the other room (reminiscent of the Showjumping World Championships). An additional prize for brilliance is awarded by Sammy Kehela, the famous Canadian international player who assists with the commentary, and me.

Strategy and Tactics

Both this book and the TV series, which runs for fourteen instalments, display similarities and differences between the type of bridge played in the average rubber game and that performed by experts. Perhaps the greatest difference in the two is that the expert has a different psychological approach to the game. He, or she, invariably has a well developed 'killer instinct', not only to penalize the opponents but also to intervene during the auction phase of the game in an attempt to buy the contract, or merely to make life difficult. The paramount objective is to win by outscoring the opponents, and to achieve this any risk is justified (well, almost!).

As well as light opening bids, one-level overcalls will also be made on seemingly flimsy hands. This is particularly true of 1 S overcalls when an opponent opens with one of a minor suit. The aim largely is obstructive, to shut out the left hand opponent if possible and especially to make it difficult for him to respond cheaply in hearts, the other major suit. Remember no trumps and the major suits are the cheapest form of game – nine tricks and ten respectively. Two other objectives are always present when overcalling. One is to suggest a sacrifice to partner should the opponents reach a contract which is likely to be made, and the second is to help partner to find

4

the best lead. Another example of the killer instinct is the expert's free use of penalty doubles. This is the only way, apart from redoubling, of trying to intimidate opponents. They must not be encouraged to overcall frivolously and should instead be punished for any indiscretion. On occasions, as will be seen, the doubler comes off worst, but that is only to be expected when one has a hair trigger deterrent.

Improving Your Game

Average players can learn much from studying the bidding, play and defence of experts. They can also gain by increasing their tactical awareness. There is, however, no better way for average players to improve their game than by practising, preferably against better players. In rubber bridge it is a good idea to play for slightly higher stakes than normal. It is amazing how careless players mend their ways when their own cash is at stake. Furthermore, it is usually worthwhile for tournament players to play cut-in rubber bridge for reasonable stakes. Only then will they realize that their methods are perhaps unsound, especially when the lessons learned cost money!

NICOLA GARDENER
December 1982

The Participants

Mrs Rixi Markus

In terms of experience and achievement, pride of place must be accorded to Rixi Markus. She was born in Vienna and won the first two European Women's Championships in 1935 and 1936, and the Women's World Championship in 1937. She became a British citizen after World War II and formed with Mrs Fritzi Gordon what was probably the greatest partnership ever seen in women's bridge. They won the World Women's Pairs Championships in 1962 and 1974, the World Women's Team Olympiad in 1964, and the Mixed Teams Championship in 1962 partnered by my father, Nico Gardener, and Boris Schapiro. Rixi also represented Great Britain in many European Championships, winning in 1951, 1952, 1959, 1961, 1963, 1966 and 1975. In Las Palmas in 1972 she became the first woman ever to attain the World Bridge Federation rank of Grandmaster. Other notable successes include the Gold Cup, partnered by Fritzi Gordon, and the Master Pairs, partnered by Michael Wolach.

Here, largely in her own words, is a résumé of her life in bridge:

It is difficult for me to give the exact date when I commenced playing bridge. I can, however, remember winning Dutch florins while on holiday in Holland with my uncle when I was twelve years of age. When I returned to Austria my father found out and I was severely reprimanded and sent off to school. At eighteen I took up playing again in Vienna in coffee-houses.

After marrying a bridge player about twice my age I had considerable opportunity for playing social bridge, but I also enjoyed competing in tournaments with Dr Hirschler, an excellent player, who taught me a great deal. Our success brought us to the attention of

Dr Paul Stern, the vice-president of the Vienna Bridge Club, the home of the Austrian Bridge Federation. In 1934 Dr Hirschler and I won a big charity event and consequently I was invited by Dr Stern to join the Austrian ladies' team which won the European Championships in 1935 and 1936, and the World Championship in 1937 in Budapest. We were going to Oslo in 1938 to defend our title when Hitler invaded Austria, so the team disintegrated and I escaped to Great Britain.

I continued playing bridge in London through the war years and afterwards, but as I was not a British citizen until 1951 I could not represent this country. With the late Lady Rhodes, whom I consider to have been a great player, we were members of the team which won the European Championship in 1951 in Venice, and in 1952 in Dun Laoghaire. In 1955 I played for the first time with Fritzi Gordon in Amsterdam, and we had many successes together in the ensuing years until I gave up playing internationally in 1976.

I have been honoured on many occasions. I have won the Charles Goren Award for Bridge Personality of the Year 1975, and I am an honorary member of the International Bridge Press Association. I was also named in the *Guinness Book of Records* as number one woman player in the world. I have been the bridge correspondent for the *Guardian* since 1955 and have written for *Harper's and Queen* and other publications, and for the *Evening Standard* before it amalgamated with the *Evening News*. Many of my books have appeared outside Great Britain, sometimes in foreign languages.

The most outstanding event in my bridge career was the day when Her Majesty the Queen pinned the MBE on my lapel and said in her lovely voice, 'You are the lady who plays bridge so well'. The citation read: 'For services to bridge'.

Unfortunately Rixi did not provide me with any hands which she played particularly well, but that was no problem. Here is one from the British Bridge League Trials of many years ago:

Dealer: North
North–South vulnerable

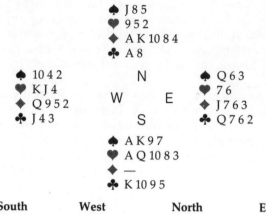

♠ J 8 5
♥ 9 5 2
♦ A K 10 8 4
♣ A 8

♠ 10 4 2
♥ K J 4
♦ Q 9 5 2
♣ J 4 3

♠ Q 6 3
♥ 7 6
♦ J 7 6 3
♣ Q 7 6 2

♠ A K 9 7
♥ A Q 10 8 3
♦ —
♣ K 10 9 5

South	**West**	**North**	**East**
Rixi Markus	*Kathy Garfield*	*Fritzi Gordon*	*Pat Forbes*
—	—	1 ♦	Pass
2 ♥	Pass	3 ♦	Pass
4 ♣	Pass	4 ♥	Pass
4 ♠	Pass	5 ♣	Pass
6 ♥	Pass	Pass	Pass

Many players would not have bid beyond game with the South hand. Up to this point the hands seemed not to fit very well. Rixi, however, is not one to give up easily, hence her slam try of 4 S. Fritzi Gordon, North, was quite justified in cue bidding the ace of clubs (a cue bid is a try for a slam, generally showing a first-round control i.e. ace or void in the suit bid), but South should have then signed off with 5 H. Fritzi might still have bid the small slam but it is very doubtful.

The slam is not a good proposition, especially as we can see that the king, jack of trumps lie badly, but Rixi has brought home worse contracts than this. The ♦ 2 was led and ruffed. The ♠ A K were cashed in the hope that the queen would drop. When it didn't Rixi continued with a club to dummy's ace. The ♦ A K were cashed, on which two losing spades were discarded. A low diamond was then ruffed. The ♣ K was cashed and a club ruffed. A spade ruff followed and now each player had but three cards left:

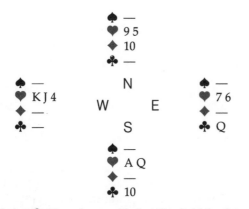

```
              ♠ —
              ♥ 9 5
              ♦ 10
              ♣ —
    ♠ —          N          ♠ —
    ♥ K J 4              ♥ 7 6
    ♦ —     W    E    ♦ —
    ♣ —          S          ♣ Q
              ♠ —
              ♥ A Q
              ♦ —
              ♣ 10
```

Rixi led the ♣10 and poor Kathy Garfield had to surrender.

If she ruffed low, dummy would overruff, and if she ruffed high, she would have to lead into Rixi's ace, queen of hearts.

Rixi Markus has enjoyed considerable success over the years when partnered by her great friend Mrs Joan Durran. Here is a deal which I published in *Now!* magazine in April 1981. I watched Rixi play it in Brighton in the 1980 final of the National Women's Championship.

Dealer: South
Love all

```
              ♠ 8 3 2
              ♥ A 4
              ♦ 10 8 6 2
              ♣ A Q 8 2
    ♠ 9 6          N          ♠ A J 7 4
    ♥ Q 10 8              ♥ J 7 5 2
    ♦ A J 9 4   W    E    ♦ 7 5
    ♣ K 10 7 4      S          ♣ J 6 5
              ♠ K Q 10 5
              ♥ K 9 6 3
              ♦ K Q 3
              ♣ 9 3
```

South	West	North	East
Rixi Markus		*Joan Durran*	
1♠	Pass	2♣	Pass
2 NT	Pass	3 NT	All pass

West led the ♦ 4. Rixi played dummy's eight which held the trick. The ♠ 2 was led to the king, West signalling a doubleton with the nine. It is not usually a good idea to signal when Rixi is declarer – she has a habit of intercepting signals and turning them to her advantage. This was no exception.

The ♣ 9 was led and ducked round to East's jack. The ♥ 2 was returned, so Rixi allowed West to win with the eight. The ♥ Q was continued, taken by dummy's ace, and a spade led to South's queen. The ♦ K was led which West won. The ♥ 10 came back so declarer won with the king. The ♦ Q was cashed and then the ♣ 8 was finessed and a diamond played. West won, cashed a second diamond, but then had to lead a club. Rixi, of course, finessed the queen and claimed nine tricks by cashing the ace of clubs.

Rixi is renowned for her adventurous bidding. Terence Reese, who was a member of the last British team to win the World Championship in 1955, invented the term 'Rixi Bids' when describing some of her more hazardous efforts. Here is an example which he described one Sunday many years ago in his *Observer* column. It occurred in the individual event at Deauville. For starters here is Rixi's hand:

♠ J 9 3
♥ —
♦ 10 8 7 6 5 2
♣ A J 10 9

She was sitting South, and West dealt at love all and opened 1 S. Her unknown partner bid 2 H and East said 3 C. Can you guess what Rixi bid? 3 D, which West doubled and all passed. Here is the full deal with the auction repeated in tabular form:

Dealer: West
Love all

```
              ♠ Q 6
              ♥ K Q J 9 5 3
              ♦ J 4
              ♣ K 7 2
  ♠ K 10 8 7 5       N        ♠ A 4 2
  ♥ A 8 7 2                    ♥ 10 6 4
  ♦ K Q 9'3      W     E       ♦ A
  ♣ —                          ♣ Q 8 6 5 4 3
                     S
              ♠ J 9 3
              ♥ —
              ♦ 10 8 7 6 5 2
              ♣ A J 10 9
```

South	West	North	East
—	1♠	2♥	3♣
3♦	Double	All pass	

The ♥ A was led. This was unfortunate for the defenders, but not fatal because there were still six top losers. Rixi, however, summed up the position like lightning. She ruffed the ♥ A and led the ♣ J. West saw little point in ruffing a loser, so he discarded a spade. Dummy's ♣ K was played and the ♥ K Q were cashed on which two losing spades were discarded. Another heart was led and East also saw no point in ruffing, so another losing spade went away. The ♣ 10 was then finessed. West ruffed and led a spade. Rixi ruffed and played the ♣ A. West ruffed and led a trump to East's ace. West, however, could not regain the lead in time to draw dummy's ♦ J so Rixi used it to ruff her last club. In all she lost but four trump tricks.

The winner of the Deauville individual tournament that year? Need you ask – Rixi Markus!

Mrs Jane Priday

Mrs Jane Priday was an automatic choice for British women's teams between 1961/71, during which period she won all the highest international honours. She does not play much bridge these days but her occasional 'outings' in top tournaments show that she has lost little of her competitive edge. She and her husband Tony, bridge correspondent of the *Sunday Telegraph*, are both ranked World Masters.

Here, in her own words, are her career details:

I began playing bridge at the age of nineteen. Until then my main interest had been riding. I owned a lovely mare named Mystery and won many prizes with her, including some for showjumping. When she developed a diseased bone in her foreleg and had to be put down I was heartbroken. I decided I didn't want another horse and would give up riding altogether. I felt I should take up another hobby to fill the gap and thought I would have a go at bridge. This was not such an unlikely choice as it sounds, because I come from a bridge playing family, although up till then I had taken no interest in the game.

In retrospect I suppose I learned fairly quickly. As I then lived in Nottingham it seemed natural to start by playing the Nottingham One Club system, but I soon changed to good old-fashioned Acol. It was not long before I represented the county and achieved a number of minor successes in local events and congresses.

In 1959 I moved to London. I first played in ladies' trials in 1961 and qualified for the team to play in the European Championship that year.

I was a member of the winning team in the following:

European Championship 1961 partnered by Dorothy Shanahan
European Championship 1963 partnered by Dorothy Shanahan
European Championship 1966 partnered by Joan Durran
World Team Olympiad 1964 partnered by Dorothy Shanahan

and Joan Durran and I won the World Olympiad Women's Pairs in 1966. After this win with Joan, I was holder of all three titles at the same time.

For a time Joan and I had a great run of success together. Possibly our best effort was in the Life Masters' Pairs in 1966 when we finished second. It was more of a quality event then than it is now – that year it was won by John Collings and Jonathan Cansino.

Also, Joan and I were invited to play in the *Sunday Times* competition in 1967. I believe only four women's pairs have ever competed in this event. Mercifully we did not disgrace ourselves, finishing a little below average.

I have not competed in women's bridge since 1971.

The major tournaments in Great Britain which I have won are:

Gold Cup
Crockford's Cup
Hubert Phillips Bowl

Spring Foursomes
Two Stars
Whitelaw Cup

Tony and I are the only married couple to have won the Gold Cup playing together. I have twice been selected, with Tony, to play for England in Camrose matches. These were against Scotland, and England won both matches.

I play comparatively little bridge nowadays. When I do play it is nearly always with Tony – and occasionally with Martin Hoffman. I am afraid I get more pleasure from completing a difficult crossword puzzle than I do from making a coup at the bridge table!

This hand occurred in my first European Championship – Torquay in 1961. It was the last match of the Championship, against the Irish ladies. We were in the lead, but the Swedes were breathing down our necks. Dorothy Shanahan was North and I was South.

Dealer: East
Love all

```
                    ♠ A Q J 8 6 5
                    ♥ A Q
                    ♦ J
                    ♣ A K 8 2
   ♠ K 10              N            ♠ 9 7
   ♥ K 10 8 7 4                     ♥ J 6 5 3 2
   ♦ A 9 6 2      W       E         ♦ K 10 8 7 4
   ♣ Q 5                            ♣ 7
                     S
                    ♠ 4 3 2
                    ♥ 9
                    ♦ Q 5 3
                    ♣ J 10 9 6 4 3
```

Third-in-hand West opened 1 H; Dorothy forced with 2 H and East bid 4 H. Dorothy was fond of saying 'Always bid what you think you can make' so I bid 4 S which, not surprisingly, she raised to 6 S.

The Irish lady led the ace and another diamond, and, as you can see, there was nothing to the play, although I heaved a mighty sigh of relief when the spade king appeared on the second round. In the other room the hand was played in 4 S after the auction 1 H – double – 4 H – pass – pass – 4 S.

For some reason the bridge columnists went to town on this hand. Some were quite kind about it, others decidedly less so. The late

Kenneth Konstam described it as 'the most undisciplined bid I have seen in my life', while Alan Hiron called it 'macabre'. I thought the comment 'imaginative' was a fair one, and I didn't in the least object to my so-called 'youthful *joie de vivre*'.

Two decades later it still amuses me to recall the hand. Michael's cue bids were then almost unknown in England, but Dorothy and I did play the unusual no trump. It seemed to me that she would certainly hold a good spade suit and probably diamonds as well. Clearly my hand was useless in defence and I didn't want to cause Dorothy a problem by passing.

Naturally, at the time I thought 4S was a 'master bid'!

Jane is modest about her successes but luckily I found a hand which she played many years ago. Here it is:

Dealer: North
Game all

```
                    ♠ A 8 6 5 2
                    ♥ K
                    ♦ A 9 4
                    ♣ Q 10 9 3
    ♠ —                  N              ♠ Q J 10 9 3
    ♥ 10 9 7 4 3                        ♥ Q 8 5
    ♦ 10 6 2        W       E           ♦ 7 5
    ♣ J 7 6 5 4          S              ♣ K 8 2
                    ♠ K 7 4
                    ♥ A J 6 2
                    ♦ K Q J 8 3
                    ♣ A
```

A reasonable contract of 6 S was bid out but, when East unwisely doubled, Jane removed to 6 NT with the South cards. East doubled but not so enthusiastically.

The ten of hearts was led and Jane was faced with the problem of finding two extra tricks. At trick two she came to hand with a diamond and led a low heart. East won and led the ♠ Q. Declarer won with the king and cashed the ♥ A and was pleased to see the queen fall. The contract was then assured because East was bound to have the ♣ K for his double. The diamonds were cashed arriving at this ending:

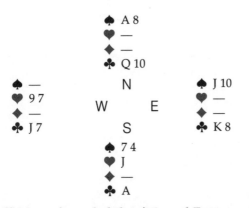

	♠ A 8	
	♥ —	
	♦ —	
	♣ Q 10	
♠ —	N	♠ J 10
♥ 9 7		♥ —
♦ — W		E ♦ —
♣ J 7	S	♣ K 8
	♠ 7 4	
	♥ J	
	♦ —	
	♣ A	

On the ♥ J Jane discarded the ♠ 8, and East was finished, caught in the toils of a merciless criss-cross squeeze. If he discarded the ♣ 8, declarer would cash the ♣ A and dummy would be high. Alternatively, if he discarded a spade, declarer would lead a spade to the ace and return to hand with a club in order to cash the ♠ 7.

Here is Jane in action more recently in 1980 in a Philip Morris European Cup heat held in London:

Dealer: North
Game all

	♠ 9 7 5 4	
	♥ J 9 6	
	♦ —	
	♣ K Q 9 8 6 2	
♠ 8 3 2	N	♠ —
♥ K 8 3 2		♥ 10 7 5
♦ A K 9 6 3	W E	♦ Q 8 7 5 2
♣ 4	S	♣ J 10 7 5 3
	♠ A K Q J 10 6	
	♥ A Q 4	
	♦ J 10 4	
	♣ A	

South	West	North	East
Jane Priday	—	*Tony Priday*	—
—	—	Pass	Pass
2 ♠	Pass	3 ♣	Pass
3 ♥	Pass	4 ♦	Pass
4 ♠	Pass	5 ♠	Pass
6 ♠	Pass	Pass	Pass

It looks as though the Pridays had missed 7 S and that is just the time for declarer to be extra careful.

A number of players in 6 S tried for an overtrick by ruffing the ♦ A lead and coming to hand with the ♠ A. A diamond ruff and a club to the ace permitted another diamond ruff. Now when the ♣ K was played West was able to ruff and return a trump or a diamond. Eventually West had to make the ♥ K to defeat the contract.

Jane, however, won the ♦ A by ruffing and crossed to hand with the ♠ A. She then unblocked the ♣ A and drew trumps ending in dummy. Two diamond losers went on the ♣ KQ. When the clubs did not break 3–3 she had to lose a heart to West's king but she had made her contract in some comfort. She could afford the luxury of finessing the ♥ Q hoping that East had the ♥ K doubleton.

Jeremy Flint

When I asked Jeremy for details of his bridge life for this book he gave me a description of himself written some fifteen years ago by Terence Reese. Here it is with additions from various sources to bring it up to date.

With long fair hair and a high thin nose he could put on a top hat and look like an Edwardian man-about-town. Flint's love of fine wine and racing add to the impression of a dilettante. But his approach to bridge is academic. He is a theorist whose many contributions to bidding systems include the Flint–Pender system, the product of his successful collaboration with the American master player Peter Pender on his tour of the States in 1966. Flint's game has sometimes been considered as too clinical or too detached, but his pragmatic ability at the rubber bridge table is a fair refutation of this criticism.

Flint is recognized as one of the most successful players on both sides of the Atlantic. He has represented Great Britain in every World Team Olympiad in which Britain has taken part, winning a silver medal and two bronze medals. He was a member of the last British team to win the European Championship in Baden–Baden in 1963, and he has represented his country in seven European Championships. His many successes include all the major domestic championships, and events in Europe, America and the Far East. He is a Grandmaster and American Life Master (which he achieved in a record ten weeks) and a World Master of the World Bridge Federation.

Today Flint plays less tournament bridge, preferring to devote his time to his new bridge interests: the organization of bridge tournaments and the operations of his new company, *Bridge Incorporated*;

and, of course, to his responsibilities as Bridge Correspondent of *The Times*.

Jeremy, who, according to the *Official Encyclopaedia of Bridge*, was born in 1928, also originated the Flint Convention for use in response to an opening bid of 2 NT (in its simplest form 3 D is a transfer to 3 H and responder either passes, or bids 3 S which opener must pass).

Here is a hand from the 1975 European Championships held in Brighton where Great Britain finished third.

```
                  ♠ A 8 6 3
                  ♥ 4
                  ♦ A 10 9 5
                  ♣ K Q J 7
   ♠ Q 7            N            ♠ J 10 5 2
   ♥ J 8 7                       ♥ K Q 9 6 2
   ♦ J 8 6 3     W     E         ♦ K
   ♣ 10 8 6 3       S            ♣ A 5 4
                  ♠ K 9 4
                  ♥ A 10 5 3
                  ♦ Q 7 4 2
                  ♣ 9 2
```

Jeremy Flint was sitting South, declarer in 3 NT after East had bid hearts. West led the ♥ 7 and declarer ducked the queen. East continued with the ♥ 2 and Jeremy went up with the ace, blocking the suit. A club to the king and ace was followed by a heart to the jack and a second club. Dummy won and Jeremy laid down the ♦ A and then ran the ♦ 10 to West's jack. The defenders had now won four tricks. West exited with a club. A diamond was discarded from hand. The ♦ Q was cashed and dummy entered with a spade to the ace. The last diamond squeezed East in the major suits. This was the ending:

```
                  ♠ 8
                  ♥ —
                  ♦ 9
                  ♣ 7
   ♠ Q             N            ♠ J 10
   ♥ —                          ♥ K
   ♦ 8          W     E         ♦ —
   ♣ 10            S            ♣ —
                  ♠ K 9
                  ♥ 10
                  ♦ —
                  ♣ —
```

Here is another delightfully simple conception, this time from the European Championships in Estoril in 1970. It occurred in the match between Great Britain and France:

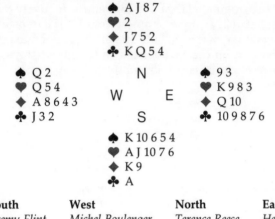

```
                    ♠ A J 8 7
                    ♥ 2
                    ♦ J 7 5 2
                    ♣ K Q 5 4
   ♠ Q 2              N          ♠ 9 3
   ♥ Q 5 4                       ♥ K 9 8 3
   ♦ A 8 6 4 3     W     E       ♦ Q 10
   ♣ J 3 2            S          ♣ 10 9 8 7 6
                    ♠ K 10 6 5 4
                    ♥ A J 10 7 6
                    ♦ K 9
                    ♣ A
```

South	West	North	East
Jeremy Flint	*Michel Boulenger*	*Terence Reese*	*Henri Svarc*
—	Pass	Pass	Pass
1 ♠	Pass	2 ♣	Pass
2 ♥	Pass	4 ♠	Pass
5 ♣	Pass	5 ♥	Pass
6 ♠	Pass	Pass	Pass

In his younger days, Jeremy used to play the Drury Convention, hence Terence Reese's bid of 2 C. Opposite a major suit opening bid a passed hand bids 2 C to ascertain whether his partner has a sound opening bid. Its main advantage is third-in-hand but Jeremy and Terence never missed the opportunity to trot out a gimmick. When Jeremy bid 2 H, and not the conventional reply of 2 D to show weakness, Terence went on to game and the partnership reached a slam, as did, in fact, the French in the Closed Room. First, let us see how the play went in that room. West, Jonathan Cansino, led the ♦ A and continued with a diamond. Jean-Louis Stoppa won with the king, crossed to dummy with the ♠ A and finessed the ♠J for one down.

In the Open Room, after a similar opening lead of the ♦ A and a diamond continuation, Jeremy cashed the ♥ A and ruffed a heart. Then came the master ♦ J. Henri Svarc mistakenly ruffed and that was that!

Finally, a hand from the 1973 English Bridge Union's Spring Foursomes which demonstrates his flawless technique:

Dealer: West
East–West vulnerable

```
              ♠ A Q 10 9 5
              ♥ 9 5
              ♦ 3
              ♣ 10 8 6 5 3
  ♠ K 4            N          ♠ J 7 3
  ♥ A Q 10 6 2                ♥ J 8 4
  ♦ K 7 4       W     E       ♦ Q 10 9 8 5 2
  ♣ Q J 9          S          ♣ 2
              ♠ 8 6 2
              ♥ K 7 3
              ♦ A J 6
              ♣ A K 7 4
```

South	West	North	East
—	1♥	2♥	Pass
4♠	Pass	Pass	Pass

North's bid of 2 H (Michael's cue bid) showed a weak hand with both black suits, so Jeremy (South) jumped to 4 S. West led the ♣ Q, which declarer won. He finessed the ♠ Q and laid down the ♠ A. The ♦ A was cashed and a diamond was ruffed. A club was led and East discarded, there was no point in ruffing a loser. Jeremy won and ruffed his losing diamond and conceded a club trick to West. He was endplayed and had to cash the ♥ A and return a heart. Jeremy won and played clubs, East making only his master trump.

Martin Hoffman

Martin was born in Czechoslovakia. When he was ten, soon after the outbreak of World War II, his parents were taken away to a concentration camp and never seen again. Martin spent about two years hiding in the mountains but was then captured and spent the last three years of the war in various concentration camps including Auschwitz. Liberated by the United States Army in 1945, he was adopted by them as a mascot and came to England in August of that year.

After a period of rehabilitation he found work in London as a diamond cutter. While living with a family in Finchley he was taught to play whist and therefore his first experience of cards was at the comparatively mature age of nineteen. He was fascinated by them and eventually discovered his true *métier* when some Russian friends introduced him to bridge. In his spare time he started going to leading clubs where rubber bridge was played and in the early 1960s he became a bridge host at the Green Street Club. Now he fills a similar role at the New Acol Club in East Finchley.

In 1965 he played in his first duplicate tournament but he is today recognized as one of the world's leading match-point pairs players. His reputation is particularly high on the Continent where he has played and won many times with Joe Moskal, Paul Hackett, Nuri Paksad and Colin Simpson. He is consistently in the annual prize money list of the Philip Morris European Bridge Cup for international pairs. Here are three of his hands:

Dealer: South
Love all

```
                    ♠ K 2
                    ♥ A K 9
                    ♦ K 10 9 2
                    ♣ K J 10 4

  ♠ 10 7 4            N            ♠ 8 6 5 3
  ♥ 7 6 3                          ♥ 5 4 2
  ♦ J 5          W       E         ♦ Q 4 3
  ♣ A Q 8 5 3        S             ♣ 9 7 6

                    ♠ A Q J 9
                    ♥ Q J 10 8
                    ♦ A 8 7 6
                    ♣ 2
```

South	West	North	East
Martin Hoffman		*Rixi Markus*	
1 ♦	Pass	3 ♣	Pass
3 NT	Pass	4 ♦	Pass
4 ♠	Pass	4 NT	Pass
5 ♥	Pass	6 ♦	All pass

Well, if you bid like that you have to play very well indeed. The occasion was a pairs tournament in Deauville and after the lead of the ace of clubs, prospects were not good. West continued with a heart so Martin took his three tricks in the suit. He then cashed two spade tricks and ruffed a winning spade in dummy. Then came the ♣ K and a club ruff. This left:

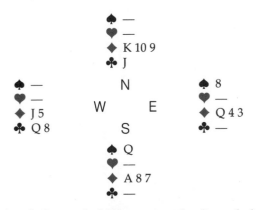

```
              ♠ —
              ♥ —
              ♦ K 10 9
              ♣ J
    ♠ —          N          ♠ 8
    ♥ —                     ♥ —
    ♦ J 5    W     E        ♦ Q 4 3
    ♣ Q 8       S           ♣ —
              ♠ Q
              ♥ —
              ♦ A 8 7
              ♣ —
```

When the ♠Q was led West correctly discarded a club. Martin ruffed in dummy and led the ♣J and the defenders' sure trump trick disappeared into thin air!

Another hand from Deauville:

```
              ♠ K Q J 6
              ♥ K Q J
              ♦ A Q 9 6
              ♣ A 6
    ♠ 9 4         N          ♠ 7
    ♥ 10 9 8 4 3             ♥ 7 6 5
    ♦ 10 3   W     E         ♦ K J 5 2
    ♣ 10 5 4 2    S          ♣ K Q J 7 3
              ♠ A 10 8 5 3 2
              ♥ A 2
              ♦ 8 7 4
              ♣ 9 8
```

For once Martin Hoffman (South) was content to stay in a modest game of 4 S. Many players reached 6 S and after the lead of the ♦10 were defeated because the slam was apparently unmakeable. They should have asked Hoffman! He covered the initial lead with dummy's queen so East won and switched to the ♣K. Hoffman won and drew trumps and on the third round of hearts he discarded a diamond. The ♦A was cashed and the ♦9 played for a ruffing finesse. East covered, but it mattered not, declarer ruffed, crossed to dummy and discarded his losing club on the ♦6.

On the next deal only two declarers made the no trump game in the Philip Morris European Cup final in Biarritz in 1977, and needless to say one of them was Martin Hoffman!

Dealer: South
East–West vulnerable

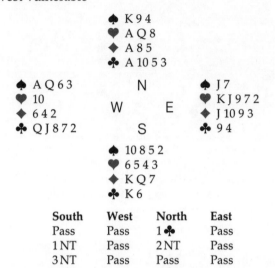

South	West	North	East
Pass	Pass	1 ♣	Pass
1 NT	Pass	2 NT	Pass
3 NT	Pass	Pass	Pass

West led the ♣ 7 and when dummy's ten held the trick the first hurdle was overcome – there were now seven top tricks. A diamond to the king allowed him to lead a low spade and play the king – and then there were eight! Returning to hand with the ♣ K he cashed the ♦ Q and ♦ A. The position was then:

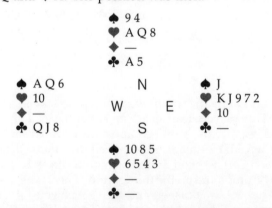

The ♠ 9 was led and West had to overtake his partner's jack to avoid the endplay in hearts. The ♣ Q was returned. Hoffman knew almost for certain that West had a 4–1–3–5 shape so he won the ♣ A, cashed the ♥ A and exited with the ♣ 5 and then there were nine!

West won but he had to concede the last trick with the ♠ 6 to declarer's ten.

Zia Mahmood

Zia was born in Karachi in 1946. He was educated in England from the age of six to twenty-one and his cultured accent owes much to his public school, Rugby. He qualified as a Chartered Accountant of the Institute of England and Wales and spent three years running the family newspaper chain in Pakistan. He also spent eighteen months in Abu Dhabi developing business interests. Although he still retains shareholdings in businesses in both Pakistan and Abu Dhabi he has retired to a life of leisure with the emphasis, and here I quote him, on bridge and women. (Note the order in which he places these two pursuits!)

He spends much of his time in Great Britain and is very much part of the London bridge scene, where he can usually be found playing high stake rubber bridge. He is extremely gifted at rubber bridge and has an incredible knack of bringing the best out of his partners. In international bridge he rates as one of the world's outstanding players and much of Pakistan's excellent performance in recent years has been due to the playing prowess of the Zia Mahmood–Masud Saleem partnership. To quote the official daily bulletin of the 1981 World Championships held in Port Chester, New York, where Pakistan finished second to the USA, 'None of his team mates can come anywhere near his brilliance and experience. His flair and daring have made his name a household word in world bridge.'

On this note it is convenient to state that Zia's most satisfying bridge experience was in reaching the Bermuda Bowl Final. During the preliminary round robin qualifying tournament he played his most interesting hand – for which he was awarded the Bols Brilliancy Prize runner-up. Here is the hand:

Dealer: South
East–West vulnerable

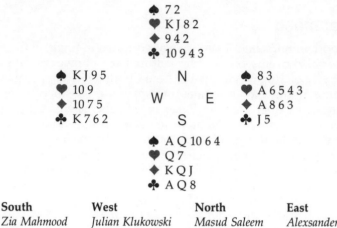

```
                        ♠ 7 2
                        ♥ K J 8 2
                        ♦ 9 4 2
                        ♣ 10 9 4 3
        ♠ K J 9 5            N            ♠ 8 3
        ♥ 10 9                            ♥ A 6 5 4 3
        ♦ 10 7 5        W        E        ♦ A 8 6 3
        ♣ K 7 6 2                         ♣ J 5
                            S
                        ♠ A Q 10 6 4
                        ♥ Q 7
                        ♦ K Q J
                        ♣ A Q 8
```

South	West	North	East
Zia Mahmood	*Julian Klukowski*	*Masud Saleem*	*Alexsander Jezioro*
2 NT	Pass	3 ♣	Pass
3 ♠	Pass	3 NT	All pass

Zia Mahmood's opening bid of 2 NT was aggressive but that is only to be expected of a player capable of making as many tricks as possible, and a few more besides. North's 3 C bid was conventional and attempted to find a major suit fit. When this was not forthcoming he settled for the nine-trick contract and allowed Zia to get to work with seemingly inadequate tools.

Julian Klukowski led the ♥10 showing either an interior sequence or the 10–9 doubleton. To quote Phillip Alder the journalist who reported this hand in the daily bulletin and thereby earned a similar Bols Award, '. . . This lead gave Zia the key to the hand. Why would West lead a heart when the dummy was almost certainly going to have four hearts? The only answer seemed to be that West had no more attractive lead. Zia decided West was holding several key honour cards.' Accordingly he played low from dummy at trick one and won with the queen when East withheld his ace. Look at the ghastly state of the contract, dummy was now as dead as the proverbial dodo. Zia, however, rose to the occasion and at trick two he led the ♠ Q! West won with the king and switched to the ♦7. The latter is a typical high spot card lead by experts when they wish to inform partner that they hold nothing in the suit. East, however, made the mistake of winning with the ace. When Zia followed with an honour a diamond was returned to declarer's queen. Next came the ♥7 to the king and ace, followed by a third round of diamonds. Zia won and now sacrificed his other black queen by leading her. This was the position:

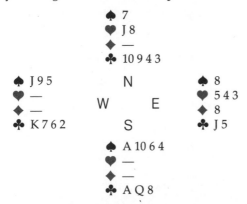

```
                    ♠ 7
                    ♥ J 8
                    ♦ —
                    ♣ 10 9 4 3
   ♠ J 9 5            N           ♠ 8
   ♥ —                            ♥ 5 4 3
   ♦ —           W       E        ♦ 8
   ♣ K 7 6 2           S          ♣ J 5
                    ♠ A 10 6 4
                    ♥ —
                    ♦ —
                    ♣ A Q 8
```

To beat the hand, West has to duck this trick. Then the best declarer can do is to play two more rounds of clubs, West wins with the king and exits with the nine of spades. He must then make the ♠ J to defeat the contract.

West, however, did take the trick with the ♣ K. He exited with a club and Zia saw that he did not need to find that East had started with the ♣ J doubleton. He put up dummy's ten, won the jack with the ace and played a club to dummy's nine. He then cashed the ♥ J, ♥ 8, squeezing West down to the singleton ♠ J, which he duly dropped at trick twelve to make exactly nine tricks.

Zia, partnering Rob Sheehan, won the 1981 English Master Pairs Championship. Here is a hand from that event:

Dealer: South
Game all

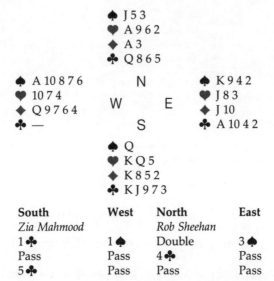

```
                      ♠ J 5 3
                      ♥ A 9 6 2
                      ♦ A 3
                      ♣ Q 8 6 5
    ♠ A 10 8 7 6        N          ♠ K 9 4 2
    ♥ 10 7 4                       ♥ J 8 3
    ♦ Q 9 7 6 4     W     E        ♦ J 10
    ♣ —                            ♣ A 10 4 2
                      S
                      ♠ Q
                      ♥ K Q 5
                      ♦ K 8 5 2
                      ♣ K J 9 7 3
```

South	West	North	East
Zia Mahmood		*Rob Sheehan*	
1 ♣	1 ♠	Double	3 ♠
Pass	Pass	4 ♣	Pass
5 ♣	Pass	Pass	Pass

Rob Sheehan's double of 1S was not for penalties. Competition
players employ the double here in a negative sense. All that it states
is that West, by reason of his overcall, has prevented North from
responding 1 H. Experts believe that frequency of occurrence justifies using the double in this sense. Note, however, that West does
not have a free licence to intervene on tram tickets. North can
always pass with a spade stack because South will reopen the bidding by doubling for take-out which North will happily convert to
penalties by passing.

As it went, East made life difficult by pre-emptively jumping to
3 S. This silenced Zia but despite his lack of aces he still went on to
game when his partner indicated club support.

The ♠ A was led and East unwisely signalled encouragement
with the nine. A spade was continued so Zia played dummy's jack
forcing East to cover with the king. Declarer ruffed and played the
♣ K. East won with the ace but the 4–0 trump break was a set-back
and when East returned the ♦ J prospects looked most precarious.
Zia, however, was unperturbed, he won in dummy with the ace and
drew trumps. Three rounds of hearts finishing in dummy produced
this ending:

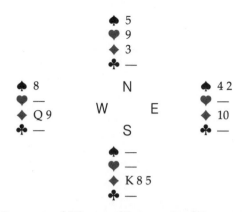

North: ♠ 5 ♥ 9 ♦ 3 ♣ —
West: ♠ 8 ♥ — ♦ Q 9 ♣ —
East: ♠ 4 2 ♥ — ♦ 10 ♣ —
South: ♠ — ♥ — ♦ K 8 5 ♣ —

The ♥ 9 squeezed West and he was forced to part with the ♠ 8 but the eagle-eyed Zia was well aware that the ♠ 5 was now master (most of us would have missed that), so he cashed it before returning to hand with the ♦ K for his eleventh trick.

Despite this brilliant play by Zia there are two tips for the average player to learn from this deal. First, East should have taken more care not to squander the ♠ 9 at trick two because when the ♠ J was played his partner was left in sole control of the spade suit. Secondly, once he had made that mistake he should have returned a spade when he won the ♣ A to remove the threat.

Here is Zia again in action, this time in a London heat of the Philip Morris European Pairs Cup competition.

Dealer: South
Love all

North: ♠ 10 9 7 6 ♥ K 7 ♦ J 3 2 ♣ A Q 8 7
West: ♠ Q 8 5 ♥ Q J 8 6 ♦ Q 10 8 5 ♣ 10 2
East: ♠ K 4 3 2 ♥ 4 3 2 ♦ 9 6 4 ♣ J 4 3
South: ♠ A J ♥ A 10 9 5 ♦ A K 7 ♣ K 9 6 5

South	West	North	East
Zia Mahmood		*Rob Sheehan*	
1♣	Pass	1♠	Pass
3NT	Pass	4♣	Pass
4♦	Pass	4♥	Pass
6♣	Pass	Pass	Pass

West led a trump so dummy's queen was played. A spade was led to the jack and queen. Another trump was led. Zia won in hand, cashed the ♠ A and crossed to dummy with the ♣ A. The ♠ 10 was led and the ♠ K ruffed, establishing the ♠ 9. A heart to the king left this position:

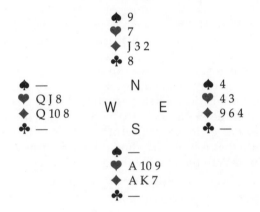

The ♠ 9 was cashed and Zia discarded the ♦ 7. West was caught in a trump squeeze. Zia would set up his twelfth trick in whichever red suit West discarded.

Irving Rose

Irving was born in Glasgow in 1938, and first played bridge at the age of thirteen, but played more later at university when aged seventeen. His mother and father were good players – the former won the Scottish Cup in 1936. He therefore grew up in an atmosphere of bridge.

He married Annette Rye in August 1981 (having been engaged for fourteen years!). Annette is known affectionately as the 'Moo'; she does not play bridge but practises astrology when Irving is playing cards. She hates the stuffy atmosphere of bridge tournaments, but nonetheless is happy to accompany Irving to the more interesting venues such as Deauville, St Moritz and Hong Kong.

Irving has won nearly every national bridge tournament; to name a few: the Spring Foursomes (a staggering seven times), Crockford's Cup (twice), and the Lederer Memorial Trophy (four times).

Internationally, perhaps it is his versatility that is most striking – his ability to play well with many partners. These have included Terence Reese, Alan Hiron, Jonathan Cansino, Jeremy Flint and Robert Sheehan. In partnership with Jeremy Flint, Irving won the Bronze Medal in the 1976 Olympics. The result of that particular competition was in doubt until the very last day and Great Britain was unlucky not to win the Silver or even the Gold. The achievement that gives Irving most pleasure is, in partnership with Robert Sheehan, finishing second in the 1981 European Championship, thus earning the right to compete in the Bermuda Bowl – incidentally the first time Great Britain had qualified for eighteen years.

His one main regret is that he has never won the prestigious Gold Cup. Apart from that, his only other regret is that as a lover of gourmet food and wine he is not a true expert in vintage wine.

Irving is most dangerous when looking for a swing. The scene was the 1981 British Bridge League international trials – it was the sixth board of an eight board match and Irving knew it was about level. That was no good if he and Robert Sheehan were to qualify.

To give you the problem, your partner opens with 3 C at favourable vulnerability (a weak bid showing a seven-card suit and not more than seven points), the next hand passes; what would you bid on the following hand?

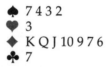

```
♠ 7 4 3 2
♥ 3
♦ K Q J 10 9 7 6
♣ 7
```

You know the opponents have at least a game – perhaps a slam – but even knowing that information, guess what Irving bid? Five Clubs (obviously intending to retreat, if doubled, to 5 D. The next hand doubled, partner passed, and 5♥ is bid on your right. What now? *Six clubs* from Irving (trying to persuade the opponents to go to 6 H). 6 H from the next hand and all passed. Robert Sheehan led the *ace of clubs*, and paused. After great consideration (Robert never plays a card without enormous thought), he led another club which Irving trumped. Irving's operatics on that board are a good illustration of his genius.

Here is a deal which I published in my column in *Now!* magazine in 1980. It occurred in an international pairs tournament and shows Irving and Rob Sheehan bidding their way carefully to a good slam in the days when they played the Precision Club System.

Dealer: South
Game all

```
                    ♠ J 9 8 7 5 4
                    ♥ A Q 7 2
                    ♦ 6
                    ♣ 6 4
  ♠ Q 10 3 2            N              ♠ K 6
  ♥ 9 6 5 4                            ♥ 8
  ♦ K 9 8        W         E           ♦ J 10 7 5 4 3
  ♣ J 8                 S              ♣ 10 9 7 5
                    ♠ A
                    ♥ K J 10 3
                    ♦ A Q 2
                    ♣ A K Q 3 2
```

South	West	North	East
Rob Sheehan		*Irving Rose*	
1♣	Pass	1♠	Pass
2♣	Pass	2♦	Pass
2♥	Pass	4♦	Pass
5NT	Pass	7♥	All pass

1 C was unlimited and showed at least sixteen points. The 1 S response was natural and positive indicating at least a five-card suit but 2 D was conventional showing less than four controls (ace counts as two controls, and a king as one). 2 H was natural and 4 D conventional showing heart support and a singleton or void diamond. 5 NT was the Josephine Grand Slam Force and requested partner to bid 6 H or 7 H depending upon whether he had one or two top honours in trumps.

After a heart lead Rob Sheehan still had a little work to do but he was equal to the task. He won the initial lead in dummy and played a diamond to the ace and ruffed a diamond. A club was his re-entry and another diamond was ruffed. A second club was played to the king and a low club ruffed with the ♥Q. Declarer returned to hand with the ♠ A to draw trumps and claim his well bid and well played contract.

At Brighton in the 1975 European Championships Irving was part-nered by Jeremy Flint. Here is one of their most spectacular hands:

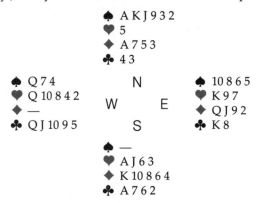

♠ A K J 9 3 2
♥ 5
♦ A 7 5 3
♣ 4 3

♠ Q 7 4
♥ Q 10 8 4 2
♦ —
♣ Q J 10 9 5

N
W E
S

♠ 10 8 6 5
♥ K 9 7
♦ Q J 9 2
♣ K 8

♠ —
♥ A J 6 3
♦ K 10 8 6 4
♣ A 7 6 2

West led the ♣ Q against Irving's 6 D contract. He won and crossed to dummy with the ♦ A and discovered the bad news. The ♠ A, ♠ K were cashed and two club losers discarded. A spade ruff brought down the queen. The ♥ A and a heart ruff allowed declarer to get to dummy where the ♠ J was cashed, on which his last club was discarded to leave this ending:

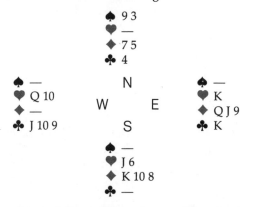

♠ 9 3
♥ —
♦ 7 5
♣ 4

♠ —
♥ Q 10
♦ —
♣ J 10 9

N
W E
S

♠ —
♥ K
♦ Q J 9
♣ K

♠ —
♥ J 6
♦ K 10 8
♣ —

A club ruff was followed by a heart ruff and when dummy led a winning spade, East could do no better than ruff with an honour. Irving discarded his losing heart and claimed the last two tricks.

Here is another one of Irving's hands from the 1976 Olympiad held in Monte Carlo, in the match Great Britain versus Israel.

Dealer: East
Game all

```
                    ♠ Q J 7 2
                    ♥ A K 10 6
                    ♦ A Q 9 6
                    ♣ K
   ♠ A 6 5 4          N           ♠ 9 3
   ♥ J 8 7 2                      ♥ 5
   ♦ 10 8 5 2      W     E        ♦ K 7 4 3
   ♣ 10               S           ♣ Q 9 8 6 5 2
                    ♠ K 10 8
                    ♥ Q 9 4 3
                    ♦ J
                    ♣ A J 7 4 3
```

South	West	North	East
Irving Rose	*Schmuel Lev*	*Jeremy Flint*	*Pinhas Romik*
—	—	—	Pass
Pass	Pass	2♦	Pass
2 NT	Pass	4♦	Pass
6♥	Pass	Pass	Pass

The bid of 2 D was an example of the so-called Multi-coloured convention and could indicate many types of hands. Irving's 2 NT was positive and expressed a willingness to play in game even if partner had a weak hand with either major suit. 4 D showed a strong hand with 4–4–4–1 shape including a singleton club. Irving then bid what he thought he could make!

The ♠ A was led and the suit continued. Irving won with the king and led the ♦ J to the ace and ruffed a diamond. At the table a player of Irving's calibre 'knows' from the reactions, even of the two Israeli champions, who has the ♦ K. The ♥ Q was cashed and a club led to the king. Another diamond was ruffed. The ♣ A was played and West discarded a diamond. Irving also discarded a diamond, the queen, leaving this end position:

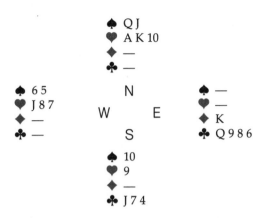

```
              ♠ Q J
              ♥ A K 10
              ♦ —
              ♣ —
♠ 6 5          N          ♠ —
♥ J 8 7                   ♥ —
♦ —       W       E       ♦ K
♣ —            S          ♣ Q 9 8 6
              ♠ 10
              ♥ 9
              ♦ —
              ♣ J 7 4
```

West's hand was counted; he had to hold all the remaining trumps, so Irving finessed the ♥ 10, drew trumps and claimed twelve tricks!

Omar Sharif

Now of Paris, formerly of Egypt, motion picture star Omar Sharif, according to the *Official Encyclopaedia of Bridge*, was born in 1932. He represented the United Arab Republic in the World Olympiad 1964, and he was playing captain of Egypt in the World Olympiad 1968. His National wins include Inter-clubs 1960, 1962, 1963, 1964. He was the winner of the 1963 Golden Globe award, and was nominated for an Academy Award in 1963 for best supporting actor in *Lawrence of Arabia*. He is one of the most active promoters of bridge, making many public appearances on syndicated television shows as a proponent of the game. He organized and headed from 1967 the Sharif Bridge Circus, a touring professional team of world-class players, to play a series of exhibition matches against leading European and North American teams. In 1970, on its second tour, the Circus (Omar Sharif, Georgio Belladonna, Benito Garozzo, Leon Yallouze and Claude Delmouly) were challenged by Jeremy Flint and Jonathan Cansino, representing the Crockford's Club, to a match over 100 rubbers in London. The stakes were probably the highest ever played, £1 a point, plus £1,000 for each set of four rubbers. The Circus won an attenuated match of eighty rubbers, with Claude Rodrigue substituting for Jeremy for part of the event, by 5,470 points. In London in 1973 he was made joint second favourite at 8–1 and went on to win the Ladbroke Club Individual Invitation Championship from a star-studded field of international players.

He won the International Bridge Press Association Simon Award for Sportsman of the Year in 1974. He is a member, with many former members of the Italian Blue Team, of the Lancia Bridge Team, playing exhibition challenge matches in New York, Chicago, Los Angeles and Miami in 1975. He currently has a bridge column in the *Sunday Express*.

Omar has played on many occasions in the British Bridge League's International Pairs event sponsored by the *Sunday Times* and finished second in 1971, partnered by Benito Garozzo. In recent years, including 1981, when it was sponsored by *Now!* magazine, he has played with Paul Chemla, one of the reigning World Olympic Teams Champions from France. In the 1981 event, the last time it was held, he finished fourth.

Like many of the participants in this televised event, Omar did not produce any hands which he has played. Here, however, is one I discovered which he played with Rixi Markus in the Sheraton Mixed Pairs Tournament in Brussels, 1973:

Dealer: South
Game all

```
                    ♠ K8765
                    ♥ 763
                    ♦ 54
                    ♣ 972
    ♠ A               N          ♠ 109
    ♥ K104                       ♥ AQ985
    ♦ J7632        W   E         ♦ K98
    ♣ AJ108           S          ♣ 654
                    ♠ QJ432
                    ♥ J2
                    ♦ AQ10
                    ♣ KQ3
```

South	West	North	East
1 NT	Pass	2♥	Pass
2♠	Pass	Pass	Pass

By opening a strong no trump with the South cards, Omar prevented West from competing (many East–West pairs made nine tricks in hearts, occasionally ten). Furthermore, the transfer sequence (2 H over 1 NT requires partner to bid 2 C) meant that South became declarer and was saved from an immediate club attack. With the

♣ A sitting over the king it still looks as though eight tricks is declarer's limit. West led the ♠ A and switched to a diamond, the king losing to the ace. Omar went to dummy by overtaking the ♠ Q and led a heart. West won with the king and returned a heart to East's ace. A third heart was mistakenly played and Omar was in control. He ruffed with the ♠ J, crossed to dummy with a trump and led a club to the king and ace. West returned a club. Omar won and cashed dummy's trumps. On the last, West had to bare the ♦ J in order to keep the ♣ 10. So Omar made the last two tricks with the ♦ Q 10 for a top score.

This was the ending:

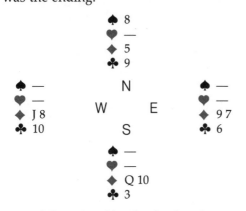

Here is one of Omar's rubber bridge hands:

Dealer: West
North–South vulnerable + 60

```
                    ♠ K J 10 5
                    ♥ 6 4 2
                    ♦ 7 5 3
                    ♣ J 4 2
    ♠ 9 4 3 2            N            ♠ 8 6
    ♥ Q 9                             ♥ A 10 8 3
    ♦ Q 9 6 2        W       E        ♦ J
    ♣ Q 8 3                           ♣ A K 10 9 7 5
                        S
                    ♠ A Q 7
                    ♥ K J 7 5
                    ♦ A K 10 8 4
                    ♣ 6
```

35

South	West	North	East
—	Pass	Pass	1♣
Double	Pass	1♠	2♣
2♦	3♣	3♦	4♣
4♦	Double	All pass	

The ♣Q was led and held the trick. A second club was ruffed by declarer. The ♦A was cashed, dropping East's jack – this looked ominous. The ♠7 to the ten followed and a low heart led from dummy. When East dropped the three, Omar made the excellent play of the king to block the suit. Three rounds of spades were cashed and a heart discarded. A club was ruffed and the position which Omar had visualized was created:

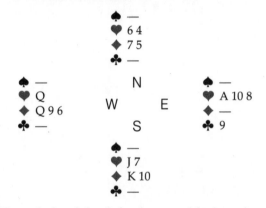

The ♥7 was led and the defenders would take only two tricks. If the ♥Q was overtaken and a club played, declarer merely discards the ♥J because West has to ruff and return a trump!

Finally here is a hand he played in New York's Cavendish Club Individual Championships in 1978:

Dealer: North
Game all

```
                    ♠ A 10 8 7 4 3
                    ♥ A J 4 2
                    ♦ 7
                    ♣ Q 6
   ♠ K J 9 6 2           N           ♠ —
   ♥ 8 7 3                            ♥ 10 6 5
   ♦ J 6            W       E         ♦ A Q 10 9 5 4
   ♣ A 10 5               S           ♣ J 8 7 2
                    ♠ 5
                    ♥ K Q 9
                    ♦ K 8 3 2
                    ♣ K 9 4 3
```

South	West	North	East
—	—	1♠	Pass
2♣	Pass	2♠	Pass
3NT	Pass	Pass	Pass

Despite playing five-card majors, Omar (South) decided to play in
3 NT and how right he was. The ♥8 was led which Omar took in
hand with the king. Ten points in hearts were too many and
therefore the hands did not fit very well. The ♠Q was led, covered
by West and ducked in dummy. East showed out discarding the ♦
10. How would you fancy Omar's chances? The ♦J was led and
ducked all round. The ♦6 was continued to East's ace. The ♥6 was
returned. As East had not cleared the diamond suit the ♣A had to
be with West, so declarer led the ♣3 and played dummy's queen.
A heart to hand left this position:

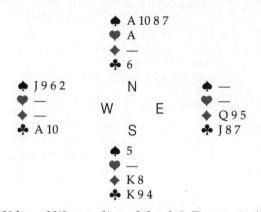

```
              ♠ A 10 8 7
              ♥ A
              ♦ —
              ♣ 6
  ♠ J 9 6 2        N         ♠ —
  ♥ —                        ♥ —
  ♦ —        W       E       ♦ Q 9 5
  ♣ A 10        S            ♣ J 8 7
              ♠ 5
              ♥ —
              ♦ K 8
              ♣ K 9 4
```

The ♦ K forced West to discard the ♠ 2. Dummy's ♠ 7 was likewise discarded. The ♠ 5 was played and the eight finessed. The ♥ A now forced West to discard the ♣ 10. The ♣ 6 endplayed him for another spade finesse.

Rob Sheehan

I will leave Rob to write his own biographical details and come in again at the end with three famous deals in which he was concerned.

I was born on 18 April 1939, and educated at Boston Grammar School and Balliol College, Oxford. I spent the years 1957 to 1969 in universities of one sort or another, getting a BA degree in Animal Physiology and then a D.Phil. The years 1964 to 1968 I spent in the USA, doing research in physiology. From 1969 to 1972 I was employed by Scicon Ltd, a firm of management consultants, mostly doing computer programming and systems analysis connected with defence projects. From 1972 to 1976 I played bridge and backgammon for a (rather poor) living. From 1976 to the present I have been employed by IG Index Ltd, of which I am a director and shareholder. Its principal business is taking bets on the price of commodities.

In August 1981 I married Penelope Cobbold. She is a personnel consultant, and a keen bridge and backgammon player.

I learned to play bridge in 1957, while I was at Oxford. Two strong players in Oxford in those days were Jonathan Cansino and Michael Buckley. I played with both on and off until I went to the USA in 1964.

When I returned from the USA in 1968, Jonathan was playing with Jeremy Flint and Michael had dropped out of bridge in order to run the country from the Treasury. I teamed up with Chris Dixon, and in 1971 we were selected to play in the European Championship in Athens. The rest of the team was Cansino, Flint, Tony Priday and Claude Rodrigue with Louis Tarlo as non-playing captain.

The British team came second to the Italians, with a percentage score that would have won in many other years.

The British Bridge League selected the 1971 European team *in toto* for the 72 Olympiad. The British team finished sixth.

Also in 1972 Chris and I won the Gold Cup in partnership with Jane and Tony Priday and Maurice Esterson and David Edwin. In 1973 and 1974 I played in the European Championships in Ostend and Herzlia with Irving Rose; we finished eighth and seventh respectively. In 1974 Rose and I were fifth in the World Pairs Olympiad in Las Palmas, having won the qualifying stage. In 1975 I played with Willie Coyle in the European Championships held in Brighton, with Priday and Rodrigue and Flint and Rose. We were third. In 1976 the same team played in the Monte Carlo Olympiad, and finished third.

I did not play in the trials in 1977 or 1979. In 1980 Flint and I, with Priday and Rodrigue, won the BBL trials, and along with Forrester and Smolski played in the Olympiad in Holland. We finished sixth in our group, and did not make the play-offs.

In 1981 Rose and I won the BBL trials, playing with William Pencharz and Raymond Brock. The selectors in fact selected the whole of the team that was second (John Collings, Paul Hackett, Tony Sowter and Stephen Lodge) along with Rose and myself to play in the 1981 European Championship in Birmingham, with Terence Reese as non-playing captain. The British team came second to Poland just ahead of the French. As a result the British team qualified to play in the 1981 Bermuda Bowl in Rye, New York.

For the Bermuda Bowl the selectors chose the whole of the Birmingham team. However the World Bridge authorities objected to Reese as non-playing captain and, amid great debate, the selectors decided to send the team with Gus Calderwood substituted as captain. The end of the unfortunate episode, in which nobody emerged with great credit, was that the British team finished an undistinguished fifth out of seven teams. The event was won by the USA with Pakistan second.

Rob Sheehan modestly supplied but one deal in which he was concerned, and furthermore he understated its importance so I have tried to redress the balance.

It occurred in the 1981 European Championships, held in Birmingham. With two rounds to go Poland were already the overall winners but Great Britain and France were fighting it out, neck and neck, for the runners-up position with a prize of a trip to New York for the Bermuda Bowl at stake. This was the second board in a remarkable match:

Dealer: East
North–South vulnerable

```
                    ♠ K 8 4 2
                    ♥ K J 4 3
                    ♦ 10 6 4
                    ♣ Q 2
  ♠ Q J 7 6 3          N            ♠ 10 9
  ♥ 9 7 5                           ♥ Q 8 6
  ♦ 8 5           W       E         ♦ K Q 9 7 3
  ♣ J 9 4              S            ♣ A 10 8
                    ♠ A 5
                    ♥ A 10 2
                    ♦ A J 2
                    ♣ K 7 6 5 3
```

In the Open Room East opened 1 D and South, John Collings, became declarer in 3 NT. He received a spade lead, which he won in hand and played a club to the queen and ace. East returned a spade which held the trick. Now East continued with a low diamond to dummy's ten. John tested clubs and, when they broke 3–3, he had nine tricks without touching hearts. As Patrick Jourdain reported in the *Daily Bulletin*, declarer is always likely to succeed for, if he has to tackle hearts, he will probably collect four tricks in the suit by finessing through the bidder. It needs a spectacular defence to set the contract and that is what Rob, sitting East, found at the other table. This was the auction:

South	West	North	East
—	—	—	Pass
1 NT	Pass	2 ♦	Double
3 ♣	Pass	3 ♦	Pass
3 NT	Pass	Pass	Pass

South's bidding showed 16–17 points and no four-card major. West led the ♦ 8 and Sheehan ducked, forcing declarer to take the jack early. Now declarer played a club to the queen and Sheehan ducked! The declarer was convinced that West had the ♣ A so he continued the suit by playing low from both hands. West won and played another diamond which was ducked but the third round, perforce, was taken. It seemed quite safe to declarer to play another club but the roof fell in!

Note that if Rob had taken the ♣ A at trick two, declarer can make an Avoidance Play to prevent him from obtaining the lead in clubs. The ♣ 2 is led and, if East plays the eight declarer ducks the trick to West. Should East instead play the ♣ 10 declarer wins with the king, and leads another club forcing West to take the trick.

With such sparkling play it is a matter of record that Great Britain overwhelmed Poland 131–39 imp's to win 20 to minus 1 but they still had to beat France. This was the critical board from that encounter:

Dealer: West
North–South vulnerable

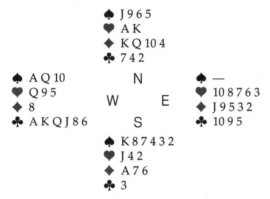

```
              ♠ J 9 6 5
              ♥ A K
              ♦ K Q 10 4
              ♣ 7 4 2
♠ A Q 10          N          ♠ —
♥ Q 9 5                      ♥ 10 8 7 6 3
♦ 8        W         E       ♦ J 9 5 3 2
♣ A K Q J 8 6     S          ♣ 10 9 5
              ♠ K 8 7 4 3 2
              ♥ J 4 2
              ♦ A 7 6
              ♣ 3
```

In the Open Room John Collings and Paul Hackett defended 5 C doubled and took 300. Here is the auction from the Closed Room.

South	West	North	East
	Irving Rose		*Rob Sheehan*
—	1 ♣	Pass	Pass
1 ♠	3 NT	Double	4 ♣
Pass	Pass	4 ♦	All pass

Irving Rose led his singleton diamond and declarer won in dummy to lead a trump. Rob Sheehan seized his chance and discarded the ♣ 10, an unmistakable signal. West won and underled his 100 for honours in clubs so Rob won with the nine and returned a diamond for a ruff and a vital nine international match points swung to Great Britain.

The final margin in this match was only six imp's in favour of Great Britain but sufficient for the team to qualify for the Bermuda Bowl in New York.

Now let us see him in action in the Round Robin for the Bermuda Bowl. Great Britain played Poland in Round Thirteen and this was Board Seven.

Dealer: South
Game all

```
                    ♠ K Q 10 6 4 3
                    ♥ K 9 7 3
                    ♦ K 9
                    ♣ 7
    ♠ J 7 2             N           ♠ A 8 5
    ♥ J 8 5 2                       ♥ 10
    ♦ 10 2        W       E         ♦ Q J 7 5
    ♣ K Q J 10          S           ♣ A 9 8 4 2
                    ♠ 9
                    ♥ A Q 6 4
                    ♦ A 8 6 4 3
                    ♣ 6 5 3
```

South	West	North	East
Irving Rose		*Rob Sheehan*	
Pass	Pass	1 ♠	2 ♣
Double	3 ♣	Pass	Pass
3 ♦	Pass	3 ♥	Pass
4 ♥	Pass	Pass	Pass

South's double of 2 C was negative, indicating possession of a four-card heart suit. East found the best lead of the ♣ A and continued with another club. When this defence was found in another match declarer went down, but Rob sitting North handled the play very well indeed. He ruffed and led a trump to the queen. The fall of the ♥ 10 suggested that the trumps were 4–1. The critical play of leading the ♠ 9 and running it to East was made. When this card produced the ♠ A, Rob was in full control. A third round of clubs was led and ruffed. He cashed the ♥ K and led spades. West ruffed the fourth round and played another club, but declarer ruffed in dummy, drew the last trump with the ace and claimed the final two tricks.

BOARD 1   Dealer: East   North–South vulnerable

```
                    ♠ K Q 9 6 2
                    ♥ Q 7 2
                    ♦ Q 10
                    ♣ K 8 3
   ♠ 5                 N           ♠ A 7 4
   ♥ J 6                           ♥ A K 10 9 3
   ♦ J 9 8 5 2      W     E        ♦ K 6 4 3
   ♣ J 10 9 6 4        S           ♣ 7
                    ♠ J 10 8 3
                    ♥ 8 5 4
                    ♦ A 7
                    ♣ A Q 5 2
```

Possible auction

South	West	North	East
—	—	—	1 ♥
Pass	Pass	1 ♠	Pass
2 ♥	Pass	2 ♠	Pass
3 ♠	Pass	Pass	Pass

East has a reasonable opening bid of 1 H but West is too weak to respond and North then makes a protective bid of 1 S. This galvanizes South into action and he first cue bids the opponent's suit and then although his partner shows little interest, he tries again with 3 S. North with his collection of kings and queens correctly turns down the invitation.

East leads the ♥ K. As the partnership normally leads the ace from suits headed by the ace king, this lead has a conventional significance. It means that East's next lead will be a singleton. When he sees that dummy has four trumps and his partner contributes the ♥ J to trick one, he decides not to lead the ♣ 7 at trick two. Instead he cashes the ♥ A and leads another for his partner to ruff. The ♣ J is returned which is won by dummy. On the ♠ J East plays the ace and returns a spade. Declarer draws the outstanding trump and cashes the ♣ K hoping for a 3–3 break. He is disappointed to see East show out. The only real chance then is a squeeze if West also holds the ♦ K. This is unlikely in view of his pass of partner's opening bid because he has already produced the ♥ J and ♣ J. Declarer has another chance, he can play West to hold the ♦ J. Accordingly he leads the ♦ Q forcing East to cover with the ♦ K and thereby transfer the control of the diamond suit to West. Two rounds of spades are cashed and West surrenders. The end position is:

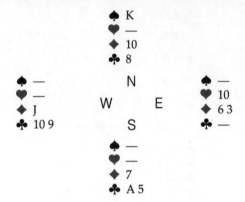

On the ♠ K dummy's ♦ 7 is discarded and West must give up a trick in one of the minor suits.

TIP When a contract looks impossible, try for a squeeze.

BOARD 1   **Dealer:** East   North–South vulnerable   Room 1

```
              ♠ K Q 9 6 2
              ♥ Q 7 2
              ♦ Q 10
              ♣ K 8 3
  ♠ 5             N          ♠ A 7 4
  ♥ J 6                      ♥ A K 10 9 3
  ♦ J 9 8 5 2  W     E       ♦ K 6 4 3
  ♣ J 10 9 6 4    S          ♣ 7
              ♠ J 10 8 3
              ♥ 8 5 4
              ♦ A 7
              ♣ A Q 5 2
```

South	West	North	East
Jane Priday	*Irving Rose*	*Rixi Markus*	*Zia Mahmood*
—	—	—	1 ♥
Pass	Pass	1 ♠	2 ♦
2 ♠	3 ♦	Pass	Pass
3 ♠	Pass	Pass	Pass

In my preview I did not forecast that East would bid again opposite a passing partner with a mere fourteen points, but it just goes to show how expert players refuse to be shut out of competitive auctions, particularly when they are not vulnerable. South's bid of 2 S is a little conservative, and personally I would bid either 2 H (a cue bid in the opponent's suit when you have passed initially shows sound support for partner's suit) or 3 S. The latter has much in its favour because it is both pre-emptive, which makes it more difficult for West to compete, and also shows that South has the values for a raise to 3 S but leaves the final decision to partner. If holding more than a minimum, North can then safely bid 4 S. 3S, however, is the contract which I wanted North to be in so we shall now see if the play and defence goes in the way I expected.

East leads the ♥ A. West signals encouragement by playing the jack, but to my surprise East switches to the ♣ 7. I see what he is trying to do; he intends to play the ♠ A on the first round of trumps, and then cash the ♥ K and lead another heart for a ruff. His partner will then win and give him a club ruff. Very clever, but how many spades does he think there are in this pack? There are four on view in dummy and East himself has three. Surely he does not think that North has overcalled 1 S on a four-card suit?

Declarer wins the club with dummy's ace and tackles spades. As I expected, East takes his ace and cashes the ♥ K and then declarer has no difficulty whatsoever in making nine tricks without any form of squeeze, for 140 (90 plus 50 for a part-score bonus). A good hand bites the dust!

```
                    ♠ K Q 9 6 2
                    ♥ Q 7 2
                    ♦ Q 10
                    ♣ K 8 3
   ♠ 5                N            ♠ A 7 4
   ♥ J 6                           ♥ A K 10 9 3
   ♦ J 9 8 5 2      W     E        ♦ K 6 4 3
   ♣ J 10 9 6 4       S            ♣ 7
                    ♠ J 10 8 3
                    ♥ 8 5 4
                    ♦ A 7
                    ♣ A Q 5 2
```

South	West	North	East
Rob Sheehan	*Martin Hoffman*	*Jeremy Flint*	*Omar Sharif*
—	—	—	1 ♥
Pass	Pass	1 ♠	2 ♦
2 ♥	2 ♠	Double	Pass
Pass	3 ♦	Pass	Pass
3 ♠	Pass	Pass	4 ♦
Pass	Pass	Pass	

So much for my preconceived ideas! Once again East decides that he cannot afford to be shut out of the auction. South's bid of 2 H unfortunately is an open invitation to West to get into the act, which he does. Furthermore, he tries to convey to his partner by cue bidding the opponent's suit that he is maximum for his initial Pass and that he has a very good hand in support for diamonds: five card trump support and a singleton spade. Such forceful bidding, however, has its reward and East is persuaded to bid again over the 3 S and succeeds in buying the contract in 4 D.

After the lead of the ♠ J declarer has very little difficulty in making ten tricks for a score of 80 plus 50 for the part score bonus, making a total of 130. This when added to the 140 which his teammates earned for making 3 S in the other room means a net plus score of 270.

Dealer: North   Love all

```
                    ♠ 8 7 6
                    ♥ 3
                    ♦ 9 6 4 3 2
                    ♣ K Q 10 3
   ♠ J 10 5            N           ♠ A 9 3
   ♥ Q J 9 8 6 4                   ♥ A K 10 7
   ♦ 5            W       E        ♦ A J 8
   ♣ A 8 6                         ♣ 9 5 2
                     S
                    ♠ K Q 4 2
                    ♥ 5 2
                    ♦ K Q 10 7
                    ♣ J 7 4
```

Possible auction

South	West	North	East
—	—	Pass	1 ♥
Pass	4 ♥	All pass	

East should open the bidding with 1 H and West raise to game. This contract when played by East is unbeatable except against the unlikely lead of a club. If West were declarer in 4 H an initial spade lead defeats the contract because the king and queen of spades are held by South.

Against the contract of 4 H by East the ♦ K is led and declarer must capitalize upon his luck in the bidding by ducking. South will then switch to a club but declarer is in full control. He wins with dummy's ace and crosses to hand with a trump. The ♦ A is cashed on which a club is discarded and then the ♦ J is played and another club discarded. This prevents North, the danger hand, from obtaining the lead. South returns a trump which declarer wins in hand in order to ruff a club. Another trump is played to regain entry so that East's last club can be ruffed. The stage is then set for declarer to lead a low spade and play the nine. Although this loses to South he is powerless to beat the contract because he is endplayed and either has to return a spade, or give a ruff–discard.

If declarer omits to duck the initial diamond lead, North can gain entry at some time with a club and by returning a spade render the endplay ineffective. Similarly if West were declarer, as well as an initial spade lead defeating the contract, the ♣ K will suffice. There is, of course, the proviso that North must switch to a spade when he is next on lead.

TIP Duck a trick when it does not cost, and can only gain.

```
                      ♠ 8 7 6
                      ♥ 3
                      ♦ 9 6 4 3 2
                      ♣ K Q 10 3
        ♠ J 10 5          N           ♠ A 9 3
        ♥ Q J 9 8 6 4                 ♥ A K 10 7
        ♦ 5           W     E         ♦ A J 8
        ♣ A 8 6          S            ♣ 9 5 2
                      ♠ K Q 4 2
                      ♥ 5 2
                      ♦ K Q 10 7
                      ♣ J 7 4
```

South	West	North	East
Jane Priday	*Irving Rose*	*Rixi Markus*	*Zia Mahmood*
—	—	Pass	1 ♥
Pass	4 ♥	All pass	

So far so good, the bidding has gone exactly as I had predicted, now I have to hope that Jane Priday will make the obvious lead of the ♦ K and that East, Zia Mahmood, finds the best line of play.

The ♦ K is led and the cards in rotation are – five, two, and wait for it, the eight! We are on course for success. Jane does well not to continue with a diamond and instead switches to the ♣ 4, Dummy's ace is played and trumps are drawn in two rounds. The ♦ A. is cashed on which one of dummy's losing clubs is discarded. Then comes the ♦ J which South has to cover but she is allowed to win this trick while dummy's second club loser is discarded. The ♣ 7 is led but Zia is in control and ruffs with the ♥ 6. He then crosses to hand with a trump so that he can ruff his remaining club in dummy. The elimination of the minor suits is complete, it does not matter any longer where the missing spade honours are. Zia leads the ♠ J and follows with the three from hand. South wins with the queen but is endplayed and has either to return a spade into declarer's major tenace, or to concede a ruff-discard.

120 for making ten tricks plus 300 bonus for the not vulnerable game means that Zia has scored 420 on this board. It now all depends upon what is to happen in the replay when his current team mates sitting North and South in Room 2, defend the same hand.

```
                        ♠ 8 7 6
                        ♥ 3
                        ♦ 9 6 4 3 2
                        ♣ K Q 10 3
        ♠ J 10 5           N           ♠ A 9 3
        ♥ Q J 9 8 6 4                  ♥ A K 10 7
        ♦ 5          W         E       ♦ A J 8
        ♣ A 8 6           S           ♣ 9 5 2
                        ♠ K Q 4 2
                        ♥ 5 2
                        ♦ K Q 10 7
                        ♣ J 7 4
```

South	West	North	East
Rob Sheehan	*Martin Hoffman*	*Jeremy Flint*	*Omar Sharif*
—	—	Pass	1 NT
Pass	2 ♦	Pass	3 ♥
Pass	4 ♣	Double	4 ♦
Pass	4 ♥	All pass	

I do not like the look of this auction despite the fact that East–West have reached the ideal contract. East's strong 1 NT opening bid is unexceptionable; it has the right shape and sixteen points. West's bid of 2 D is a transfer indicating at least a five-card heart suit. Nothing is conveyed about the diamond suit, it is merely a conventional bid, and may be very weak or the prelude to game or even a slam. East obviously regarded his hand as very suitable, because instead of merely bidding 2 H as his partner expected, he jumped to 3 H to indicate that even with a weak hand opposite there were good prospects for game. This show of strength encouraged West to make a mild slam try by cue bidding the ♣ A. Unfortunately this gave North the opportunity for a cost nothing double to inform his partner that he was not averse to a club lead. East made another mild slam try by cue bidding the ♦ A, but West had learnt enough and signed off in game. A club lead, as I stated in the preview, defeats the contract for certain, because it guarantees an entry to the North hand for a spade return which breaks up the endplay. With a safe lead of his own, however, South chooses instead to lead the ♦ K.

Declarer makes the mistake of winning this. He then draws trumps and ruffs a diamond. A low club is played from the table but North goes up with the queen in order to play the ♠8. This is ducked to the queen but South is in no difficulty and gets off play with the ♣7. Dummy's ace wins and although declarer wriggles for a little while longer, eventually he is forced to finesse the ♠J. When this loses to South he is defeated and loses 50 aggregate points.

The net score on this board is therefore plus or minus 470 aggregate points – 50 to North–South in Room 2 plus 420 achieved by their current team members sitting East–West in Room 1.

BOARD 3   **Dealer:** South   East–West vulnerable

```
                    ♠ Q J 9 8 5
                    ♥ 6 2
                    ♦ K J 8
                    ♣ 9 7 3
  ♠ A 6 3              N           ♠ 4
  ♥ K Q 10 8                       ♥ J 9 4
  ♦ A Q 5        W       E         ♦ 7 6 4 2
  ♣ J 4 2              S           ♣ A K Q 10 5
                    ♠ K 10 7 2
                    ♥ A 7 5 3
                    ♦ 10 9 3
                    ♣ 8 6
```

Possible auction

South	West	North	East
Pass	1♥	1♠	2♣
2♠	2NT	Pass	3♥
Pass	4♥	All pass	

A contract of 3NT by East–West has no chance after a spade lead. 5C is reasonable but will also fail because the ♦K is badly placed. The best contract is 4H but it requires careful trump control. After the ♠Q lead South should realize that his best chance is to overtake with the king. Standard technique for declarer in this type of contract with only seven trumps is to withhold the ace. A spade continuation can then be ruffed in the short trump hand. Trumps are played and the ace forced out because the ♠A stops the run of the spade suit and declarer readily makes eleven tricks.

South by playing the ♠K at trick one does not prevent declarer from ducking, but South will then be well placed to switch to the ♦10. This defeats the contract for certain because the defenders cannot be prevented from taking two diamond tricks.

TIP As on Board 2, declarer, despite holding the ace, must duck the opening lead, but this time to 'keep control of the hand'.

BOARD 3   Dealer: South   East–West vulnerable   Room 1

```
                    ♠ Q J 9 8 5
                    ♥ 6 2
                    ♦ K J 8
                    ♣ 9 7 3
      ♠ A 6 3           N          ♠ 4
      ♥ K Q 10 8                   ♥ J 9 4
      ♦ A Q 5       W       E      ♦ 7 6 4 2
      ♣ J 4 2                      ♣ A K Q 10 5
                        S
                    ♠ K 10 7 2
                    ♥ A 7 5 3
                    ♦ 10 9 3
                    ♣ 8 6
```

South	West	North	East
Jane Priday	*Irving Rose*	*Rixi Markus*	*Zia Mahmood*
Pass	1♥	1♠	2♣
2♠	3♠	Pass	4♠
Pass	5♣	All pass	

West's bid of 3S is quite a shock to me, but East's 4S brings a nasty feeling to the pit of my stomach – another par hand going wrong! 5C is not a bad contract, just about fifty per cent but I know that the ♦K is wrong. Why couldn't they play enterprisingly in 4H?

In my opinion West's first duty is to inform his partner of the type of hand which he holds. Presumably his system prevented him from opening a strong no trump, which is unquestionably the most descriptive call. He therefore had no choice but to open 1H, intending to rebid 1NT or 2NT depending upon the level at which his partner responded. Nothing has really changed except that the opponents have got together in spades. A slightly conservative bid of 2NT is therefore in order at West's second turn to call. Zia Mahmood would then have bid 3H (forcing in this sequence), and

51

Irving Rose would probably have raised to 4 H because he would expect to find a singleton spade opposite. As the auction went, I cannot blame Zia for calling 4 S, in context he has a good hand.

South leads the ♦ 10 and from that moment the contract is doomed, not even a chance of a mis-defence to save East–West's blushes.

BOARD 3 **Dealer:** South   East–West vulnerable   Room 2

```
                    ♠ Q J 9 8 5
                    ♥ 6 2
                    ♦ K J 8
                    ♣ 9 7 3
    ♠ A 6 3            N           ♠ 4
    ♥ K Q 10 8                     ♥ J 9 4
    ♦ A Q 5       W       E        ♦ 7 6 4 2
    ♣ J 4 2            S           ♣ A K Q 10 5
                    ♠ K 10 7 2
                    ♥ A 7 5 3
                    ♦ 10 9 3
                    ♣ 8 6
```

South	West	North	East
Rob Sheehan	*Martin Hoffman*	*Jeremy Flint*	*Omar Sharif*
Pass	1 NT	Pass	2 NT
Pass	Pass	Pass	

I might have guessed it, Martin Hoffman and Omar Sharif have agreed to play a strong no trump throughout. This makes it far more difficult for them to reach the best contract of 4 H. Normality is not helped when Omar bids 2 NT as a transfer, indicating a five–card club suit. Nadir is reached when Martin forgets that 2 NT means clubs, or to be fair, perhaps he has never been told. That is always the difficulty in an individual contest when one changes partners after every four boards. For East–West, however, this is perhaps a lucky accident because 2 NT is unbeatable even after an initial spade lead. A score of 120 plus the 100 earned by their team mates in the other room soon brings the smiles back to the East–West pair. North–South do not seem to share their joy!

BOARD 4   Dealer: West   Game all

```
                    ♠ 10 8 5 2
                    ♥ 8 5 4 2
                    ♦ A K Q
                    ♣ 8 3
   ♠ Q J 6 3              N              ♠ A K
   ♥ Q 7                                 ♥ A K
   ♦ 10 4 3        W         E           ♦ J 9 7 6 5 2
   ♣ Q J 9 5              S              ♣ A 6 2
                    ♠ 9 7 4
                    ♥ J 10 9 6 3
                    ♦ 8
                    ♣ K 10 7 4
```

Possible auction

South	West	North	East
—	Pass	Pass	1♦
Pass	1♠	Pass	3NT
Pass	Pass	Pass	

The auction on this deal is likely to be brief. South should lead the
♥ J and declarer will realize that he does not have the time to set up
his diamond suit. The only chance for nine tricks therefore is to
make three tricks in clubs. Dummy, however, has only one entry
and that is in clubs but the defenders will almost certainly withhold
the ♣ K and then only two club tricks can be made. If only dummy
had a second entry – but it has if one looks hard enough! Declarer
wins the ♥ A, cashes the ♠ A K and leads the ♣ 2, playing
dummy's queen. As expected this card holds the trick. The ♠ Q is
then cashed and the ♥ K discarded, creating dummy's second
entry. A club is then led to the ace and the club return guarantees
nine tricks. If the defenders refuse to continue hearts they will have
to play diamonds but they can only make three tricks in that suit
before declarer makes the remainder.

TIP When communications between declarer and dummy are
poor, consider ways of making your contract another way.
'Unblocking' with the help of your opponents.

♠ 10 8 5 2
♥ 8 5 4 2
♦ A K Q
♣ 8 3

♠ Q J 6 3   **N**   ♠ A K
♥ Q 7   ♥ A K
♦ 10 4 3   **W**   **E**   ♦ J 9 7 6 5 2
♣ Q J 9 5   **S**   ♣ A 6 2

♠ 9 7 4
♥ J 10 9 6 3
♦ 8
♣ K 10 7 4

South	West	North	East
Jane Priday	*Irving Rose*	*Rixi Markus*	*Zia Mahmood*
—	Pass	Pass	1 ♦
Pass	1 ♠	Pass	3 NT
Pass	Pass	Pass	

For once my predicted auction is realized. Furthermore South leads the ♥ J.

Declarer, Zia Mahmood, wins with the king and unblocks the ♠ AK. The ♣ 6 comes next and I sit back expecting to watch a master craftsman at work, but – South plays the king. Another heart is led and declarer spreads his hand, claiming nine tricks for a score of 600.

It is easy to be wise after the event but it is far more difficult to defend at the table. Rixi Markus correctly signalled at trick one with the ♥ 5 showing an even number of cards, probably four in this instance. If these four include the ace it may be necessary for South to take her king and cash the hearts before they run away. Careful analysis reveals that East cannot really have four running diamond tricks as well as the ♣ A and therefore South should withhold her ♣ K.

Another point of interest is that Zia won the first trick with the ♥ K and not the ♥ A. The latter would have been a giveaway.

```
                    ♠ 10 8 5 2
                    ♥ 8 5 4 2
                    ♦ A K Q
                    ♣ 8 3
    ♠ Q J 6 3            N           ♠ A K
    ♥ Q 7                            ♥ A K
    ♦ 10 4 3        W       E        ♦ J 9 7 6 5 2
    ♣ Q J 9 5            S           ♣ A 6 2
                    ♠ 9 7 4
                    ♥ J 10 9 6 3
                    ♦ 8
                    ♣ K 10 7 4
```

South	West	North	East
Rob Sheehan	*Martin Hoffman*	*Jeremy Flint*	*Omar Sharif*
—	Pass	Pass	1 ♦
Pass	1 ♠	Pass	2 NT
Pass	3 NT	All pass	

A slightly conservative bid of 2 NT by East but luckily West has enough to go on to game. The ♥J is led; declarer wins, and to my surprise the ♣2 is played. This cannot be correct because South will simply duck and in due course dummy might as well be consigned to the waste paper basket. South, however, has his own ideas on the subject and plays the king, in order to lead another heart. Again the difficulty may have been caused by North's signal with the ♥5 at trick one. The defence is far more difficult for Rob Sheehan to find in this room compared with that in Room 1 because the ♠ AK have not been cashed, revealing the whereabouts of declarer's high cards. As in Room 1 declarer carefully won the first trick with the ♥K and not the ace. Nine tricks are therefore made, and we have our first flat board of the contest.

This ends the first chukka of play and after comparing scores, partnerships are changed. New bidding methods, within the overall guidelines which I set, are discussed and play continues for boards 5–8.

BOARD 5   **Dealer:** North   North–South vulnerable

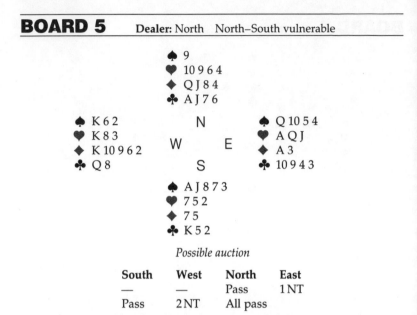

♠ 9
♥ 10 9 6 4
♦ Q J 8 4
♣ A J 7 6

♠ K 6 2
♥ K 8 3
♦ K 10 9 6 2
♣ Q 8

N
W   E
S

♠ Q 10 5 4
♥ A Q J
♦ A 3
♣ 10 9 4 3

♠ A J 8 7 3
♥ 7 5 2
♦ 7 5
♣ K 5 2

Possible auction

South	West	North	East
—	—	Pass	1 NT
Pass	2 NT	All pass	

If playing a weak no trump throughout East does well to make this bid because it prevents South from overcalling cheaply in spades. West will raise to 2 NT and there the bidding should die. If East decides to open with 1 C, South should overcall with 1 S and West may then become declarer in a no trump part score contract, but North's lead of the ♠ 9 will not be very helpful to declarer. On the other hand if East becomes declarer without bidding spades, South will almost certainly lead the ♠ 7. Declarer will win the first trick with the ten and see that his contract is virtually certain without playing on diamonds. The correct action is to return a spade immediately and play dummy's king – South cannot play his ♠ A without giving an extra trick in the suit. Declarer then has seven top tricks and an eighth is readily available if he concedes three clubs to the ace, king, jack.

TIP When a contract looks easy, pause and be sure to COUNT YOUR TRICKS.

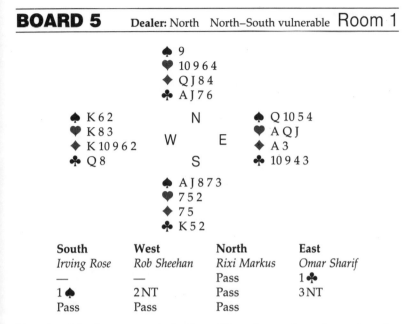

	♠ 9	
	♥ 10 9 6 4	
	♦ Q J 8 4	
	♣ A J 7 6	
♠ K 6 2	**N**	♠ Q 10 5 4
♥ K 8 3		♥ A Q J
♦ K 10 9 6 2	**W E**	♦ A 3
♣ Q 8	**S**	♣ 10 9 4 3
	♠ A J 8 7 3	
	♥ 7 5 2	
	♦ 7 5	
	♣ K 5 2	

South	West	North	East
Irving Rose	*Rob Sheehan*	*Rixi Markus*	*Omar Sharif*
—	—	Pass	1 ♣
1 ♠	2 NT	Pass	3 NT
Pass	Pass	Pass	

Yes, I might have guessed, East–West have elected to play the strong no trump, so East has to open 1 C. This allows South to make a damaging overcall of 1 S and it also creates a problem for West. He decides to show his values by bidding 2 NT, although 2 D was the response I was hoping for.

As I fear, North leads the ♠ 9. Declarer plays dummy's queen and South wins with the ace. Declarer's play of dummy's top honour card is a technique which has the object of preventing South from ducking in the hope that his partner can subsequently obtain the lead and play the suit again. Although West can reasonably place North with a singleton spade, he takes no risk, defenders have been known to overcall on a four-card suit. Having won the ♠ A, South has to find a switch and chooses to lead the ♦ 7. Declarer plays the ten, North the jack and dummy the ace. It is time for declarer to play for miracles and the first requirement is to set up a club trick so the three is led and South smartly plays the king. When this holds the trick he continues with the ♦ 5. Declarer hopefully inserts the nine but no luck, North wins with the queen. A heart comes back. Declarer wins in dummy and plays another club to the queen and North's ace. Another heart is led but this time declarer wins in hand. The ♦ K is cashed and declarer's last chance expires when South shows out, discarding the ♠ 3. A heart is led to the ace but declarer is finished and concedes three down, losing 150.

```
                      ♠ 9
                      ♥ 10 9 6 4
                      ♦ Q J 8 4
                      ♣ A J 7 6
      ♠ K 6 2            N            ♠ Q 10 5 4
      ♥ K 8 3                         ♥ A Q J
      ♦ K 10 9 6 2    W     E         ♦ A 3
      ♣ Q 8             S             ♣ 10 9 4 3
                      ♠ A J 8 7 3
                      ♥ 7 5 2
                      ♦ 7 5
                      ♣ K 5 2
```

South	West	North	East
Zia Mahmood	*Jeremy Flint*	*Jane Priday*	*Martin Hoffman*
—	—	Pass	1 NT
Pass	2 ♣	Pass	2 ♠
Pass	2 NT	Pass	3 NT
Pass	Pass	Pass	

Again I am disappointed even though East opens with a weak no
trump. West's use of the Stayman Two Club convention is a blow.
It is used to inquire about the opening bidder's four-card major suits
and therefore normally has a prerequisite for responder to hold at
least one major suit. When transfer bids are employed, however,
2 NT cannot be bid in its natural sense (it would demand 3 ♣ from
partner), and for this reason West has to resort to the Stayman
machinery. Unfortunately it has the side effect of informing South
that East has four spades and he therefore looks for another lead.
His choice is the ♥ 5.

To digress for a moment, because the lead of the five from an
original holding of 7–5–2, may appear to be strange to the
uninitiated; it is an example of the MUD Convention. MUD stands
for middle, up, down. Many players prefer to differentiate between
leading the top card from a doubleton and the top-of-nothing lead
from three small cards. By leading the middle one and later continuing with the top card they try to alert partner to the fact that their
original holding was three worthless cards. This convention is more
useful when defending a suit contract, but good players, even when
defending against no trump contracts, often try to warn their partner off returning the suit by leading the middle card.

Martin Hoffman is sitting East and after gravely thanking his partner he gets down to work. He wins the first trick with the queen. Not having any helpful bidding to guide him he decides to attack spades as the best chance of making nine tricks on seemingly inadequate values. The ♠ K wins and a spade is returned but North shows out, discarding the ♥ 4. This is a blow but Martin impassively plays the ♠ 10 which loses to the jack. The ♥ 7 is returned indicating that the initial lead was indeed MUD so Martin now knows eight of South's cards. He wins with the ace and leads a low club to dummy's eight. North wins with the jack and exits with a heart to which all follow. The ♣ Q is led and South wins with the king. Back comes the ♦ 7 so Martin covers with the nine and wins the jack with the ace. The ♣ 10 is led, forcing the ace and establishing declarer's nine. North exits with the ♣ 7. This is the end position which declarer has played for:

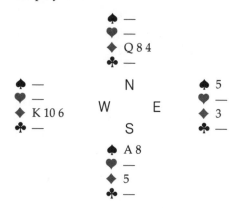

Martin leads the ♦ 3 and spectacularly plays dummy's ten. He knows that the finesse will lose but that North will be endplayed and forced to return a diamond into dummy's tenace.

This excellent piece of card reading enables Martin to get out for one down losing 50. As his opponent in Room 1 sitting West went three down in a similar contract, Martin's good play wins the board for his current team mates.

```
                    ♠ 10
                    ♥ A Q J 9 6
                    ♦ A K 10 6 5 3
                    ♣ 2
  ♠ K Q J 9 8 7 5 3    N        ♠ 6 2
  ♥ 5                           ♥ K 4 2
  ♦ J 4          W        E     ♦ Q 8 7 2
  ♣ K 10              S         ♣ A J 8 5
                    ♠ A 4
                    ♥ 10 8 7 3
                    ♦ 9
                    ♣ Q 9 7 6 4 3
```

Possible auction

South	West	North	East
—	4 ♠	4 NT	Pass
5 ♣	Pass	5 ♦	Pass
5 ♥	Pass	Pass	Pass

This is a bidding hand. West will almost certainly open 4 S. North, who can play at the five-level in either of two red suits, should invite partner's co-operation by bidding 4 NT. This is clearly a demand take-out and South should obviously choose to call 5 C. When North removes this to 5 D the spotlight will switch to South. What can North's bidding mean? The only rational reason is that North has a red two-suiter. South's action is then clear-cut and 5 H should be the final bid.

As can be seen 5 D cannot be made; in fact it should go two off, yet 6 H is a better contract being slightly below a fifty per cent chance. North–South, however, will do well to reach 5 H and be most satisfied with the outcome.

TIP While a double of an opening bid of 4 H would encourage partner to respond, a double of 4 S is for penalties. 4 NT indicates a strong hand and is for take-out showing any two suits. Partner must respond in his lowest suit, conceivably one of three cards if he has a 3–4–3–3 shape.

```
                    ♠ 10
                    ♥ A Q J 9 6
                    ♦ A K 10 6 5 3
                    ♣ 2
♠ K Q J 9 8 7 5 3       N        ♠ 6 2
♥ 5                              ♥ K 4 2
♦ J 4              W      E       ♦ Q 8 7 2
♣ K 10                 S         ♣ A J 8 5
                    ♠ A 4
                    ♥ 10 8 7 3
                    ♦ 9
                    ♣ Q 9 7 6 4 3
```

South	West	North	East
Irving Rose	*Rob Sheehan*	*Rixi Markus*	*Omar Sharif*
—	4♠	4 NT	Pass
5♣	Pass	5♦	Pass
5♥	Pass	Pass	Pass

Surprisingly, one of my more tentative long-range bidding forecasts has come off. Rixi Markus's good bid of 4 NT, indicating a two-suiter, was correctly interpreted by Irving Rose, because when she retreated from 5 C to 5 D he confidently bid 5 H. Let us see if he can make this contract.

The ♠ K is led so declarer wins with the ace and returns the ♠ 4 discarding dummy's ♣ 2. I do not like the way this is going. Declarer avoided the dummy force at trick one when a spade was led but he seems to have surrendered the initiative. I would have played the ♦ 9 to the ace and ruffed a low diamond with the ♥ 7. Even if this is overruffed it will fetch the ♥ K and I will still have a chance of success. When the diamond ruff stands up I would lead the ♥ 3 and finesse the nine. This would seem to be the best line of play and succeeds even if the trumps break 4–0 because another low diamond can be ruffed safely with the ♥ 8. Still, back to the main action.

West wins the spade and plays the ♣ 10. Declarer ruffs with the ♥ Q and cashes the ♦ AK. He is very lucky to find that these stand up. He continues with a low diamond which he ruffs with the ♥ 7. A club is ruffed with the ♥ 6 and another diamond with the ♥ 8. Yet another club is ruffed and is followed by a diamond ruffed with the ♥ 10. This is the four-card ending:

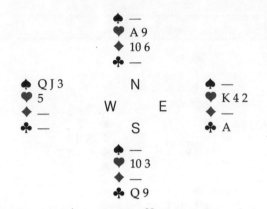

After ruffing the ♦ 6 with the ♥ 10, the ♣ 9 is led and declarer no doubt hopes that he can get this past West in order to discard the ♦ 10 and make the last two tricks. He is unlucky because West ruffs, forcing dummy to overruff, and East makes two tricks to defeat the contract and gain 50 points.

It is quite true that declarer would have succeeded if the hearts had broken 4–0 but the line of play which I have suggested above also allows for that possibility.

Declarer was also unlucky in that he committed a minor indiscretion at trick eight when he ruffed the ♦ 5 with the ♥ 8 and not the ♥ 10, even though the cards are equal in value. At trick nine when he led a club, West showed out and now it was too late for declarer to recover. At this stage West's shape is known to be 8–1–2–2 or, and less likely, 7–2–2–2. Declarer must assume the former, so he ruffs the club with the ♥ 6 and cashes the ♥ A. A winning diamond then forces East to capitulate. His best try is to ruff with the ♥ K and return a heart. Now do you see why dummy's trump has to outrank declarer's? If it doesn't, the thirteenth trick will be won by East's ♣ A and not dummy's ♦ 10.

Bridge can be a frustrating game at times, but almost invariably the old adage 'The cards never forgive' proves correct.

```
                    ♠ 10
                    ♥ A Q J 9 6
                    ♦ A K 10 6 5 3
                    ♣ 2
   ♠ K Q J 9 8 7 5 3    N        ♠ 6 2
   ♥ 5                           ♥ K 4 2
   ♦ J 4          W       E      ♦ Q 8 7 2
   ♣ K 10              S         ♣ A J 8 5
                    ♠ A 4
                    ♥ 10 8 7 3
                    ♦ 9
                    ♣ Q 9 7 6 4 3
```

South	**West**	**North**	**East**
Zia Mahmood	*Jeremy Flint*	*Jane Priday*	*Martin Hoffman*
—	4 ♠	5 ♦	Double
Pass	Pass	Pass	

A wheel has come off; North obviously thinks that a bid of 4 NT would be regarded as minor-suit orientated. So it might, but North can then remove 5 C to 5 D and hope that South can visualize North's type of hand. East's double is incredible. Opposite a partner who has pre-empted and therefore shown a weak hand what is the point of doubling? There is no guarantee of defeating the contract but more important if 5 D does go down surely that must be a good result. Trying to gild a lily may result in one of the opponents running to 5 H. How would East then feel? It was, however, East's lucky day because there followed three passes in rotation.

The ♠ 6 is led. Dummy wins with the ace and the ♦ 9 is led. Jeremy Flint carefully covers with the jack and East's stockholding soars in value.

Declarer wins the ace, cashes the ♦ K and leads the ♦ 6. East wins and subsequently makes three more tricks to defeat the contract by 300.

North–South in Room 1 will be pleasantly surprised to find that they have gained 250 on this board. Conversely East–West in that room will be bitterly disappointed with their fate.

```
                    ♠ 7 5
                    ♥ Q 10 9
                    ♦ A 6 4 2
                    ♣ A K 8 3
   ♠ K 8 4 3 2          N          ♠ A Q 9
   ♥ 8 5 3                         ♥ 7
   ♦ 10          W         E       ♦ K Q J 8 7
   ♣ Q J 7 5          S             ♣ 10 9 4 2
                    ♠ J 10 6
                    ♥ A K J 6 4 2
                    ♦ 9 5 3
                    ♣ 6
```

Possible auction

South	West	North	East
—	—	—	1 ♦
1 ♥	1 ♠	2 ♦	2 ♠
3 ♥	Pass	4 ♥	All pass

East will open 1 D and South overcall 1 H. North should cue bid 2 D to try to elicit more information from his partner. He is not quite good enough for a direct bid of 4 H opposite a one level overcall. South's very good heart suit will then ensure that game is reached.

West will lead the ♦ 10 which dummy must win. Declarer should see that he has nine top tricks and his tenth could come from a spade ruff. But he will have to lose the lead twice in spades and will be forced to ruff diamonds high. This will lead eventually to a trump promotion of East's ♥ 8.

At tricks two and three the ♣ AK are cashed and a diamond discarded. This is an obvious prerequisite to playing spades but it is not so obvious to ruff a low club at trick four. This, however, is just as essential. At trick five a spade is conceded and East wins, cashes the ♦ K and plays the ♦ Q. South ruffs high and leads another spade. East wins and again plays a diamond. South ruffs high, enters dummy with a trump and ruffs dummy's remaining club loser with the ♥ J. Ten tricks are therefore achieved by an alternative method, that of reversing the dummy.

TIP Ruffing in the long trump hand can sometimes gain.

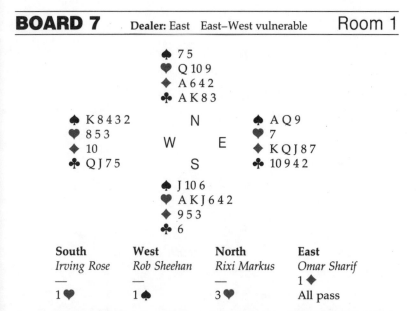

♠ 7 5
♥ Q 10 9
♦ A 6 4 2
♣ A K 8 3

♠ K 8 4 3 2   N   ♠ A Q 9
♥ 8 5 3   W   E   ♥ 7
♦ 10   ♦ K Q J 8 7
♣ Q J 7 5   S   ♣ 10 9 4 2

♠ J 10 6
♥ A K J 6 4 2
♦ 9 5 3
♣ 6

South	West	North	East
Irving Rose	*Rob Sheehan*	*Rixi Markus*	*Omar Sharif*
—	—	—	1 ♦
1 ♥	1 ♠	3 ♥	All pass

A surprising auction; it never crossed my mind that North–South could possibly stay out of game. I would prefer to bid 4 H rather than 3 H with the North hand but I still think that a cue bid is the best initial action. At least this informs partner that North has a good hand. At the favourable vulnerability there is a danger that the jump raise may be regarded as pre-emptive. Either way holding the South hand I would bid game.

The ♦ 10 is led and declarer naturally plays dummy's ace. The ♣ A is played and is followed by the ♣ K on which the ♦ 5 is discarded, and West carefully follows with the ♣ J. Then comes the ♣ 3 and my hopes soar but declarer, instead of ruffing, discards the ♦ 9. West, for some inexplicable reason, overtakes his partner's trick and kindly puts declarer back in business by returning a club. This soft defence forces declarer to ruff with a low trump – the essential play for an overtrick which he had missed at trick four. Declarer leads the ♠ J which East wins and returns a trump. This is surprising, I would have thought a diamond was best but it does not really matter, the horse has bolted. Declarer wins and leads another spade and claims ten tricks because he can safely ruff a spade in dummy and then draw trumps.

```
                    ♠ 7 5
                    ♥ Q 10 9
                    ♦ A 6 4 2
                    ♣ A K 8 3
      ♠ K 8 4 3 2         N         ♠ A Q 9
      ♥ 8 5 3                       ♥ 7
      ♦ 10         W         E      ♦ K Q J 8 7
      ♣ Q J 7 5         S          ♣ 10 9 4 2
                    ♠ J 10 6
                    ♥ A K J 6 4 2
                    ♦ 9 5 3
                    ♣ 6
```

South	West	North	East
Zia Mahmood	*Jeremy Flint*	*Jane Priday*	*Martin Hoffman*
—	—	—	1 ♦
1 ♥	1 ♠	2 ♦	2 ♠
3 ♥	Pass	4 ♥	All pass

I feel much happier after this auction because this was my suggested sequence.

The ♦ 10 is led. Declarer plays dummy's ace and continues with the ♣ A and the ♣ K discarding the ♦ 9. Unfortunately the next lead is a spade on which East thoughtfully plays the queen! He is in a great position to defeat the contract. If he cashes the ♦ K and follows with the ♦ Q declarer will have to ruff high. Another spade lead will be won by East and a fourth diamond played. Once again declarer will have to ruff high. Although he can then obtain a spade ruff and cash the ♥ Q and ♥ 10 he can only return to hand by ruffing a club. By this time West will have dispossessed himself of his clubs on the diamond leads and his ♥ 8 will be promoted.

This is wishful thinking because East returns the ♥ 7. Declarer wins in dummy and leads another spade which West wins. A heart is returned but declarer is in no difficulty, he wins in hand and ruffs a spade with the ♥ Q. A club is ruffed and the outstanding trump drawn.

North–South in this room and East–West in Room 1 therefore score a net 250 points (420 less 170).

BOARD 8   Dealer: South   Game all

```
                        ♠ 5
                        ♥ Q 9 8 2
                        ♦ 10 9 7 4
                        ♣ 9 7 4 2
      ♠ Q J 9 8 2          N              ♠ K 10 6 3
      ♥ 6 3                               ♥ J 4
      ♦ A 6 2        W         E          ♦ K Q J 8 5
      ♣ K 8 3                             ♣ A 5
                        S
                        ♠ A 7 4
                        ♥ A K 10 7 5
                        ♦ 3
                        ♣ Q J 10 6
```

Possible auction

South	West	North	East
1♥	1♠	2♥	4♠
Pass	Pass	Pass	

East–West are likely to play in 4 S although North–South may sacrifice in 5 H which goes two down if East–West can negotiate a club ruff.

Assuming that West plays in 4 S North will lead a heart to South's king. The ♦ 3 will be returned because South will see that he can obtain a diamond ruff when he wins the ♠ A. All that he will have to do will be to underlead his ace of hearts so that his partner can obtain the lead with the queen.

Declarer, however, will also be aware of the situation and he should try to interrupt the North–South lines of communication by playing three rounds of clubs discarding the ♥ J. It will then be the defenders' turn to counter-attack. This can be done by South unblocking the ♣ Q and ♣ J on the first two club leads. North should then play the ♣ 9 on the third round and South follow with the ♣ 6. This defence effectively thwarts declarer and nothing can prevent North from gaining entry in clubs or hearts for the fatal diamond ruff.

TIP When a ruff is pending, try to cut the defenders' communications.

```
                      ♠ 5
                      ♥ Q 9 8 2
                      ♦ 10 9 7 4
                      ♣ 9 7 4 2
   ♠ Q J 9 8 2          N              ♠ K 10 6 3
   ♥ 6 3                               ♥ J 4
   ♦ A 6 2          W       E          ♦ K Q J 8 5
   ♣ K 8 3              S              ♣ A 5
                      ♠ A 7 4
                      ♥ A K 10 7 5
                      ♦ 3
                      ♣ Q J 10 6
```

South	West	North	East
Irving Rose	*Rob Sheehan*	*Rixi Markus*	*Omar Sharif*
1♥	1♠	2♥	3♦
Pass	Pass	Pass	

Another bidding misunderstanding! Omar Sharif obviously intended his bid of 3D to be forcing and a mild slam try when he
subsequently jumped to 4S. Unfortunately he was never given the
opportunity. I would have thought that a six loser hand with only
one ace was not worth a slam try opposite a one level overcall –
though in mitigation to Omar, the continental style of simple overcall is far stronger. Even so, I would hesitate to bid 3D if there were
the slightest danger of Rob Sheehan passing. A cue bid of 3H must
be the safest bet.

The ♥K is led and North signals encouragement by playing the
nine. South continues with the ♥A and then switches to the ♣Q,
so declarer readily makes ten tricks by drawing trumps and then
conceding the ♠A.

Although this is a disastrous result for East–West it could have
been worse. There is a case for North signalling with the ♥Q at trick
one. This may then be read as a suit preference signal by South for
a spade switch (perhaps a little obscure, but we can only make use
of the tools we have) – North can hardly want South to underlead
his ♥A, which is the normal meaning of signalling with a queen,
in order to lead through declarer's hand. If South interprets the
message accurately and cashes the ♠A, and follows with another,
North ruffs, returns the ♥9 and obtains another spade ruff for +100
to North–South.

```
                        ♠ 5
                        ♥ Q 9 8 2
                        ♦ 10 9 7 4
                        ♣ 9 7 4 2
        ♠ Q J 9 8 2         N          ♠ K 10 6 3
        ♥ 6 3                           ♥ J 4
        ♦ A 6 2         W     E         ♦ K Q J 8 5
        ♣ K 8 3             S           ♣ A 5
                        ♠ A 7 4
                        ♥ A K 10 7 5
                        ♦ 3
                        ♣ Q J 10 6
```

South	West	North	East
Zia Mahmood	*Jeremy Flint*	*Jane Priday*	*Martin Hoffman*
1♥	1♠	2♥	4♠
Pass	Pass	Pass	

This is a better auction and I eagerly await the cut and thrust which will arise after a heart lead. South will of course win the first trick and switch to the singleton ♦ 3. His partner's ♥ Q will be the vital entry for her subsequently to obtain a diamond ruff as I have envisaged in my preview. Jane Priday leads the ♥ Q! I know now what Robert Burns meant by '. . . the best laid schemes o' mice an' men' – did it also apply to women? The imaginative lead of the ♥ Q was an attempt by Jane to retain the lead until dummy was seen. The second lead would then have been through dummy's weakness. This is occasionally the necessary technique where dummy or declarer has a singleton heart and, first-in-hand, has to maximize the value of the lead. On this hand it was catastrophic because it squandered the only card of re-entry. Nevertheless I find the cat and mouse play between Zia Mahmood sitting South and Jeremy Flint, sitting West, fascinating.

Zia overtakes his partner's ♥ Q with the ace and returns the ♦ 3 which is won in dummy with the king. Jeremy inquires of Zia whether Jane's lead of the ♥ Q was Roman. He is informed that it was not. The point of this question is that the Italian Blue Team, who were for many years World Champions, used a system of leads whereby they led the second ranking of touching honour cards. Hence, here, Jane's lead of the ♥ Q, if it were Roman, would confirm that she has the ♥ K.

Jeremy seems amused to learn that Zia must therefore have the ♥ K and so he should be because dummy's ♥ J indicated that North can have no re-entry in the heart suit.

Although he is reassured, Jeremy is too experienced a player to overlook the possibility that North may have false-carded and still have the ♥ K. Also he is a technician and finds pleasure in playing correctly. He will therefore try to discard dummy's heart on the third round of clubs if he can be certain that Zia will have to win the trick. Accordingly he cashes the ♣ A but Zia unblocks with the jack. The ♣ 5 is continued but Zia sticks to his plan and follows with the ten. Jeremy wins with the king and leads the ♣ 8. Jane is also aware of what is going on and covers with the nine. It is now not safe for Jeremy to discard the ♥ J because Zia might be able to underplay his partner's ♣ 9 and receive a diamond ruff. He therefore ruffs with the ♠ 10 and plays trumps and makes ten tricks. It was a good try by Zia and except for the disastrous lead by Jane he would have succeeded in defeating what at first glance appears to be an impregnable contract.

Jeremy also shares the credit for his expertize but what is far more meaningful he earns 490 points for his team.

Once again it is time to change partners.

```
                      ♠ Q J 9 3
                      ♥ K 7 3
                      ♦ A 8 5 2
                      ♣ Q 3
     ♠ A 7 5 2            N           ♠ 8 6
     ♥ A 8                            ♥ 10 9 6 5
     ♦ Q 10 7 6 3    W       E        ♦ J 9
     ♣ J 5              S             ♣ K 9 8 6 4
                      ♠ K 10 4
                      ♥ Q J 4 2
                      ♦ K 4
                      ♣ A 10 7 2
```

Possible auction

South	West	North	East
—	—	—	Pass
1 NT	Pass	2 ♣	Pass
2 ♥	Pass	3 NT	All pass

The probable contract is 3 NT played by South. In the possible auction set out above, North's bid of 2 C is an inquiry requesting South
to bid a major suit. When the response is not spades, North has to
settle for game in no trumps.

West will lead the ♦ 6 and East plays the jack. Normally in such
a situation declarer holds off the first trick. If the diamonds then
break 5–2 as long as the major suit aces are split the contract should
succeed. If declarer does not duck the first trick and he guesses
wrongly by playing the major suit in which East holds the ace,
another diamond lead would defeat the contract.

Such reasoning on this hand, however, is too shallow. The ♦ 6 is
presumably a fourth best lead and an expert declarer will try to
reconstruct West's diamond suit. It cannot be headed by QJ10 or QJ9
and with Q109 to five, West would probably have chosen to lead the
ten. It looks therefore as though East has QJ or J9. If this is so
dummy's ♦ 8 will serve as an intermediate stopper.

After winning trick one declarer should force out the ♠ A. This
not only guarantees three tricks in the suit but the ♦ A is the only
certain entry to dummy should the defence duck the first two
rounds of spades.

Say West wins the third round of spades and returns the ♦ 3,
declarer plays dummy's five so East wins with the nine but he

cannot then go! A club return will be ducked to dummy's queen and a heart return will also be ineffective. Nevertheless a heart exit could lead to interesting play because South should play the ♥ Q or ♥ J in order to force West's ace. The ♦ Q will be then played and won by dummy's ace. The thirteenth spade is cashed and hearts played. The suit, however, fails to break and once again South has only eight top tricks. His ninth trick becomes available because he is forced to rely on East having the ♣ K. The method is to exit with the fourth heart which East has to win and return a club. Naturally South plays low and dummy's queen wins a cheap trick.

TIP Defenders often lead fourth best in a suit. This enables partner to subtract the pip value of the card led from eleven (see p.74) and thereby calculate the number of unseen higher cards held by declarer. Such information can be intercepted, and used, as on this hand, by declarer.

BOARD 9   Dealer: East   Game all   Room 1

```
                    ♠ Q J 9 3
                    ♥ K 7 3
                    ♦ A 8 5 2
                    ♣ Q 3
      ♠ A 7 5 2          N          ♠ 8 6
      ♥ A 8                         ♥ 10 9 6 5
      ♦ Q 10 7 6 3   W     E        ♦ J 9
      ♣ J 5              S          ♣ K 9 8 6 4
                    ♠ K 10 4
                    ♥ Q J 4 2
                    ♦ K 4
                    ♣ A 10 7 2
```

South	West	North	East
Rob Sheehan	*Zia Mahmood*	*Rixi Markus*	*Martin Hoffman*
—	—	—	Pass
1♣	1♦	1♠	Pass
1 NT	Pass	3 NT	All pass

As South's system prevented him from opening with a weak no trump he opened with a suit call and rebid 1 NT. This is a very reasonable method. It has the one disadvantage that it allows an opponent, as here, to overcall cheaply at the one level. North was in no doubt on the second round and raised to game.

The ♦3 is led. Dummy's two is played and declarer pauses to consider the meaning of East's jack. With the helpful overcall it would seem right to me to win the first trick and expect dummy's ♦8 to act as a partial stopper. It is unlikely that West has the ♦Q109 and two or three small diamonds because he might have led the ♦10, the standard lead of the top of an interior sequence.

However, experts do discriminate between Q10972 and Q10932 – from the latter, it is right to lead the three if you suspect either opponent of holding four cards in the suit. Declarer, however, cannot see through the backs of the cards and decides to duck the ♦J. The ♦9 is continued, and from that moment the contract is doomed. West has two aces to be forced out and after winning the first, the ♦Q is played, not only to knock out dummy's ace, but as a suit preference signal to inform East that West's entry is in the higher ranking of the other two suits. Declarer goes one off, conceding 100.

BOARD 9   Dealer: East   Game all   Room 2

```
                    ♠ Q J 9 3
                    ♥ K 7 3
                    ♦ A 8 5 2
                    ♣ Q 3
   ♠ A 7 5 2            N            ♠ 8 6
   ♥ A 8                             ♥ 10 9 6 5
   ♦ Q 10 7 6 3     W       E        ♦ J 9
   ♣ J 5                             ♣ K 9 8 6 4
                       S
                    ♠ K 10 4
                    ♥ Q J 4 2
                    ♦ K 4
                    ♣ A 10 7 2
```

South	West	North	East
Omar Sharif	*Jane Priday*	*Irving Rose*	*Jeremy Flint*
—	—	—	Pass
1♣	1♦	1♠	Pass
1 NT	Pass	3 NT	All pass

An identical bidding sequence to Room 1. I wonder if the play will go the same way? It does, virtually card for card, so declarer subsides also to one down, and we have another flat board making a total of two in the tournament so far.

73

If declarer in either room could have been certain that West's initial lead was his fourth best diamond then the Rule of Eleven could have been applied. This so-called rule which was discovered in the days of whist states: 'Subtract the number of pips on the card led from eleven; the result gives the number of higher cards than the one led in the other three hands.' Why eleven, you might ask? Well, the lowest card in a suit is the two. Starting in ascending order from the two, the ace is mathematically fourteen. Therefore by leading the fourth highest there are three cards of greater value in the opening leader's hand, hence 14–3 gives eleven unknown cards.

BOARD 10   Dealer: North   East–West vulnerable

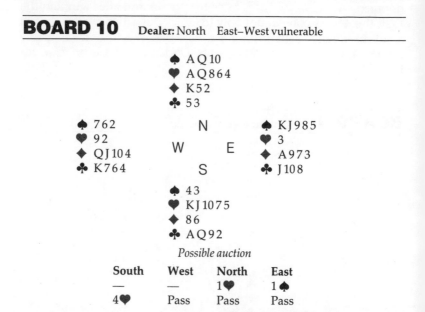

```
                    ♠ A Q 10
                    ♥ A Q 8 6 4
                    ♦ K 5 2
                    ♣ 5 3
    ♠ 7 6 2          N          ♠ K J 9 8 5
    ♥ 9 2                       ♥ 3
    ♦ Q J 10 4   W     E        ♦ A 9 7 3
    ♣ K 7 6 4        S          ♣ J 10 8
                    ♠ 4 3
                    ♥ K J 10 7 5
                    ♦ 8 6
                    ♣ A Q 9 2
```

Possible auction

South	West	North	East
—	—	1♥	1♠
4♥	Pass	Pass	Pass

The bidding is likely to be brief. North will open 1 H and East overcall 1 S. South will then simply bid 4 H closing the auction.

The ♣ J will probably be led and before playing any card declarer will review the situation. Both black kings would seem to be badly placed and, in view of his overcall, East is also likely to hold the ♦ A. There would appear to be four losers but declarer should resort to a technique known as Avoidance Play.

If the ♣ J is ducked West can only gain the lead by playing the king. This is too high a price to pay because declarer's two losing spades can then be discarded on the ♣ A Q. In that event, declarer will of course finesse the ♣ 9 playing East for the ten which is probable from his lead of the ♣ J.

Assuming therefore that East is allowed to score the ♣ J he should switch at trick two to a trump. Declarer wins in hand and leads a club to the ace and returns the ♣ Q, forcing West to cover. Declarer ruffs, crosses to dummy with a trump, cashes the ♣ 9, discarding a diamond, and then takes the finesse of the ♠ 10. East wins but he is endplayed and forced to return a spade or a diamond for declarer's tenth trick.

If, mistakenly, the ♣ Q is played at trick 1, West wins and must switch at trick two to the ♦ Q. Only by making effective use of his entries can he protect his partner from the otherwise fatal endplay.

TIP Take account of the bidding to plan safest way of making your contract.

BOARD 10   Dealer: North   East–West vulnerable   Room 1

```
                ♠ A Q 10
                ♥ A Q 8 6 4
                ♦ K 5 2
                ♣ 5 3
   ♠ 7 6 2          N          ♠ K J 9 8 5
   ♥ 9 2                        ♥ 3
   ♦ Q J 10 4    W     E        ♦ A 9 7 3
   ♣ K 7 6 4         S          ♣ J 10 8
                ♠ 4 3
                ♥ K J 10 7 5
                ♦ 8 6
                ♣ A Q 9 2
```

South	West	North	East
Rob Sheehan	*Zia Mahmood*	*Rixi Markus*	*Martin Hoffman*
—	—	1♥	1♠
4♥	Pass	Pass	Pass

Another successful bidding prediction. My luck also holds when the ♣ J is led.

Declarer Rixi Markus, however, does not find the recommended line of play by ducking the first trick. She plays the ace and draws trumps ending in hand. Her next lead is the ♣ 3 and when East plays the eight she calls for dummy's two! Rixi has recovered very well. If I had foreseen this possibility I would have given the ♣ 8 to West.

Zia Mahmood is helpless. He cannot win the trick with the king because the price is too high. This is the characteristic of a true Avoidance Play – Rixi would have two club discards for her ♠ Q and ♠ 10 and she would merely lose two diamond tricks in addition to the ♣ K – he therefore plays low but East is also in difficulty and is forced to lead the ♣ 10. Rixi covers with the queen and ruffs West's king. Dummy is entered with a trump and the ♦ 2 is discarded on the ♣ 9. The hand is practically over, Rixi has cleverly engineered an endplay which guarantees her contract irrespective of the position of the outstanding cards. Here it is:

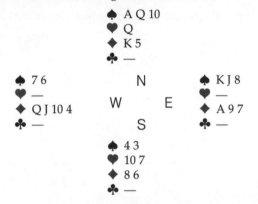

She leads the ♠ 3 and covers West's six with the ten and claims her contract. East wins with the ♠ J but he knows that he is without resource and graciously concedes ten tricks.

BOARD 10 Dealer: North East–West vulnerable Room 2

```
              ♠ A Q 10
              ♥ A Q 8 6 4
              ♦ K 5 2
              ♣ 5 3
♠ 7 6 2            N            ♠ K J 9 8 5
♥ 9 2                          ♥ 3
♦ Q J 10 4     W    E          ♦ A 9 7 3
♣ K 7 6 4          S           ♣ J 10 8
              ♠ 4 3
              ♥ K J 10 7 5
              ♦ 8 6
              ♣ A Q 9 2
```

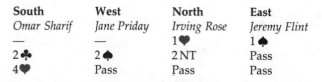

South	West	North	East
Omar Sharif	*Jane Priday*	*Irving Rose*	*Jeremy Flint*
—	—	1♥	1♠
2♣	2♠	2NT	Pass
4♥	Pass	Pass	Pass

Although it is more normal, if playing the Acol System, to raise to the limit with good support for partner's major suit opening bid, Omar's 2 C bid is well reasoned. He is in a competitive situation and by making a forcing bid to show where his outside strength lies, he may prevent partner from making a phantom sacrifice should West raise spades pre-emptively.

The ♣ J is led and again declarer makes the mistake of winning it with the ace. Trumps are drawn in two rounds and a low club is played towards dummy. This time, however, declarer makes an inferior play by covering the ♣ 8 with the nine. West wins with the king and I fully expect declarer to be punished when the ♦ Q is led to the next trick, but he is reprieved. The ♠ 7 is returned (this play was probably influenced by the ♠ 9 discard by East on the second trump) and hurriedly covered with the ten. East wins with the jack and gets off play with the ♣ 10. Dummy wins with the queen and declarer discards the ♦ 2. The ♣ 2 is ruffed and three rounds of trumps puts East under great pressure.

Here is the ending:

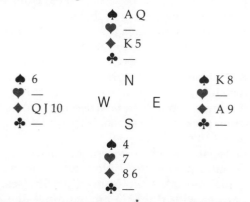

On the last trump, West discards the ♦ Q, declarer the ♦ 5, and East the ♦ 9. A diamond lead then endplays him for a spade lead away from his king into declarer's major tenace. This technique is known, for obvious reasons, as a Strip Squeeze throw-in.

Summing up, I suppose justice was done in the end with a tied board. No one really deserved to win, although Rixi Markus' line of play in Room 1, while not perfect, was clearly better than that of the declarer in Room 2.

♠ 5 2
♥ K 10 8 7 3
♦ A Q 7 5
♣ K 5

♠ K 10 4
♥ A Q 5
♦ 9 8 4
♣ A 9 6 3

                N
          W   E
                S

♠ A Q J
♥ 9
♦ J 10 6
♣ Q J 10 8 4 2

♠ 9 8 7 6 3
♥ J 6 4 2
♦ K 3 2
♣ 7

Possible auction

South	West	North	East
—	1 NT	Pass	3 NT
Pass	Pass	Pass	

East's hand has only eleven high card points but his good six-card club suit justifies his bidding game in no trumps even if his partner has a minimum. Note that it would be wrong to bid clubs because East has no intention of playing in five of that suit.

The lead is the ♥ 7 and South plays the jack. Declarer observes that his contract is safe if South has the ♣ K because he can cross to dummy with a spade and lead the ♣ Q for a finesse. But what if North has the ♣ K? He will win and seeing no future in continuing with hearts will switch to another suit and there is only one left – diamonds. This will almost certainly be fatal because, unless the suit is blocked, at least four tricks will be available to the defenders. Can nothing be done about this?

Light dawns and declarer resorts to deception. He wins trick one, not with the ♥ Q but with the ♥ A! Now when he crosses to dummy with a spade and takes the losing club finesses, North might place his partner with the ♥ Q and continue the suit by leading the ♥ 3.

North, however, may not be so ingenious. He will realize that if his partner does have the ♥ Q and two more he can afford to un-block the queen. So he may lead the ♥ K first and trust his partner to play the queen if he holds that card. When South instead plays the ♥ 2 North realizes that West is trying to fool him and switches to the ♦5, which gives him the satisfying result of a two-trick defeat.

TIP When a switch by the defence would be fatal try to resort to camouflage.

BOARD 11   Dealer: West   North–South vulnerable   Room 1

```
                        ♠ 5 2
                        ♥ K 10 8 7 3
                        ♦ A Q 7 5
                        ♣ K 5
      ♠ K 10 4            N          ♠ A Q J
      ♥ A Q 5                        ♥ 9
      ♦ 9 8 4         W     E        ♦ J 10 6
      ♣ A 9 6 3          S           ♣ Q J 10 8 4 2
                        ♠ 9 8 7 6 3
                        ♥ J 6 4 2
                        ♦ K 3 2
                        ♣ 7
```

South	West	North	East
Rob Sheehan	Zia Mahmood	Rixi Markus	Martin Hoffman
—	1 NT	2♥	3♣
3♥	3 NT	4♥	5♣
Pass	Pass	Double	All pass

Rixi Markus, sitting North, hates the weak no trump and overcalls it with impunity. South keeps the pot boiling and Zia Mahmood, West, quietly bids 3 NT which must be the final contract. Wait for it. The intrepid Rixi, vulnerable against not, bids 4 H. As the cards lie she will lose only 200 in 4 H doubled but she has the 9th Cavalry charging to her rescue from out of the East. The ♥ 2 is led but there is very little to the play. East gloomily concedes 300, realizing too late that once again Rixi Markus has persuaded an opponent to indulge in a phantom sacrifice. Cheer up, Martin, the same thing may happen in Room 2.

```
                    ♠ 5 2
                    ♥ K 10 8 7 3
                    ♦ A Q 7 5
                    ♣ K 5
    ♠ K 10 4              N              ♠ A Q J
    ♥ A Q 5                              ♥ 9
    ♦ 9 8 4         W         E          ♦ J 10 6
    ♣ A 9 6 3             S              ♣ Q J 10 8 4 2
                    ♠ 9 8 7 6 3
                    ♥ J 6 4 2
                    ♦ K 3 2
                    ♣ 7
```

South	West	North	East
Omar Sharif	*Jane Priday*	*Irving Rose*	*Jeremy Flint*
—	1 NT	Pass	2 NT
Pass	3 ♣	3 ♥	4 ♣
4 ♥	5 ♣	Double	Pass
Pass	Pass		

The bid of 2 NT is a transfer indicating a club suit. West merely rebid as instructed but this type of situation is made for Irving Rose, sitting North, and he weighed in with 3 H. East was caught; he has a good hand but, opposite a weak no trump, game was not likely so he settled quietly for a part-score. South then made a bid which when one is vulnerable can only be justified by the final outcome! West slipped from grace by unilaterally going on to 5 C and this received its just desserts. I should have thought that West could double tentatively. East can still remove it to 5 C if he is really paralytic.

North kicks off with the unfortunate lead of the ♥ 7 so I realize that declarer will be punished to the extent of only 100, but . . . ! The ♥ Q wins and the ♥ A is cashed on which a losing diamond is thrown. The ♥ 5 is ruffed. Then, for some reason which I do not follow, three rounds of spades are played. Irving ruffs the third round, cashes the ♦ A and leads another. South wins and leads a fourth round of spades so Irving scores his ♣ K *en passant*!

Lightning really does strike twice in the same place! A phantom sacrifice in both rooms conceding 300, so the board is, as the Americans say, 'a push'.

♠ 9 7 5 4
♥ J 9 65 2
♦ 7
♣ A 9 4

♠ 2   N   ♠ K Q J 10 8 6 3
♥ Q 10 7 3   ♥ A K
♦ 9 6 5 4 2   W   E   ♦ A
♣ K 5 2   S   ♣ J 6 3

♠ A
♥ 8 4
♦ K Q J 10 8 3
♣ Q 10 8 7

Possible auction

South	West	North	East
1 ♦	Pass	1 ♥	4 ♠
Pass	Pass	Pass	

South leads the ♦ K. Declarer has nine certain tricks and in view of
the bidding, the high card points are likely to be split 12–5 with
South and North respectively. Declarer's first hope is that North has
the ♠ A when South is certain to have the ♣ A. Accordingly a spade
honour is returned at trick two. Unfortunately for declarer, South
wins and continues with a diamond. North discards the ♥ 2 and
East pauses to reappraise the situation.

North must have the ♣ A. The position of the ♣ Q and ♥ J cannot
be determined for certain but they do not matter. The ♥ 2 discard
is almost certainly from a five-card suit so probably North has the ♥ J
and hence South the ♣ Q. Declarer sees the way clear and ruffs with
the ♠ 6! The ♠ Q J are cashed, followed by the ♥ A K and then
comes the *coup de grâce.*. East leads the carefully preserved ♠ 3.
North is forced to win and is endplayed. He has been stripped of all
his safe exit cards and now must return either a heart into dummy's
tenace, or a club. It matters not: declarer has cleverly converted nine
tricks into ten by first reducing them to eight.

It is probably worth stating that this recommended line of play
should be adopted irrespective of the position of the ♣ A. The obvious reason is that it guarantees ten tricks.

Note too that if declarer had carelessly ruffed the diamond with
the ♠ 3, North would have had a counter to the endplay. He simply

underplays the ♠6 leaving East on play and forced to tackle the club suit himself. There is, of course, an assumption in this line of reasoning. It is that North is not careless when he follows suit to the second spade lead. If he does not retain the ♠4 or the ♠5 he will not be able to underplay the ♠6.

TIP Don't squander your small trumps, they may have a hidden value – it often pays to 'donate' a trick to your opponents, especially when two come floating back.

BOARD 12   **Dealer:** South   Love all   Room 1

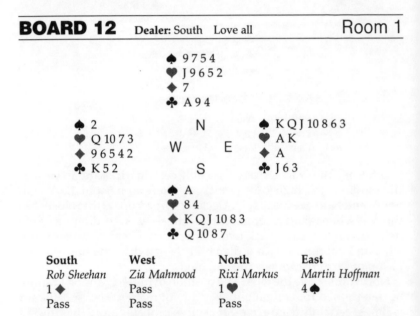

South	West	North	East
Rob Sheehan	*Zia Mahmood*	*Rixi Markus*	*Martin Hoffman*
1♦	Pass	1♥	4♠
Pass	Pass	Pass	

I have got the auction right again. Never were there such days! Rob Sheehan leads the ♦K. Declarer wins and leads the ♠K. Rob wins and as he can see all the remaining diamonds, knows that there is no future in that suit. He cleverly conceals this fact from declarer and exits with the ♥8 (I suspect trying to avoid his partner being endplayed with KJ9 to four or five hearts). North plays low and declarer wins with the ♥K. The ♠Q is played and South discards the ♦3.

At this point declarer should take time off to reconsider his problem. As I have already stated in the preview, East has eighteen points and dummy five. Assuming the opening bidder has twelve this only leaves five for North who dredged up a one level response of 1 H, presumably on a suit headed by the jack. Ten of South's points are already known and therefore, either he is missing the ♣ A, or North has responded at most on a queen and a jack, which is not very likely as his heart suit is so weak. If the ♣ A is with North, dummy's king is dead and therefore there is no entry to the ♥ Q and the contract must fail unless the ♣ Q is doubleton so that the jack can be established. This is also not very probable and declarer should then see that his only chance is to endplay North with the fourth round of trumps and make him lead into dummy.

It is, however, not to be and declarer draws trumps with the ♠ J 10. He then cashes the ♥ A, plays another round of trumps for luck and exits with a low club to the king. North wins and returns the ♣ 9. Declarer ducks, hoping for the miracle of the ♣ Q doubleton. It is not, so he concedes one down, losing 50.

It is very easy to be wise after the event. In fact I often tell my students at the London School of Bridge that the very best players are the kibitzers, especially those who sit NE, NW, SE or SW! Full marks, though, to Rob Sheehan. If he had continued with a diamond at trick three he would have informed declarer that the sit was breaking 6–1 and that a straw in the wind might have been sufficient to swing the contract the other way.

BOARD 12   Dealer: South   Love all   Room 2

```
                    ♠ 9 7 5 4
                    ♥ J 9 6 5 2
                    ♦ 7
                    ♣ A 9 4
   ♠ 2                 N            ♠ K Q J 10 8 6 3
   ♥ Q 10 7 3                       ♥ A K
   ♦ 9 6 5 4 2     W       E        ♦ A
   ♣ K 5 2            S             ♣ J 6 3
                    ♠ A
                    ♥ 8 4
                    ♦ K Q J 10 8 3
                    ♣ Q 10 8 7
```

South	West	North	East
Omar Sharif	*Jane Priday*	*Irving Rose*	*Jeremy Flint*
1♦	Pass	1♥	4♠
5♦	Pass	Pass	Double
Pass	Pass	Pass	

This was an unexpected turn up. At aggregate scoring where honours are counted I suppose that South might risk a sacrifice but, with the scoring method in use in this event, honours are not counted. Furthermore the vulnerability is equal. It is quite inexplicable to me.

Jane Priday is sitting West – note that she did not automatically double 5 D, but left the decision to her partner, Jeremy Flint. If he had a weak hand based solely upon a long spade suit she is right to pass and, if he has a strong hand with a smattering of defensive tricks, he will double at his turn to call.

Jane and Jeremy are merciless in defence. The ♠2 is led and declarer wins Jeremy's ♠K with the ace. Note the play of the ♠K in this situation. The ♠3 would have been sufficient to bring down the singleton ace, but Jeremy saw the opportunity of giving a suit preference signal. A high spade indicated an entry in the higher ranking suit. Therefore he wants a heart in preference to a club lead should his partner get in first.

Declarer leads the ♦K, Jeremy wins and plays ♠QJ10 in that order. Declarer discards two losing hearts but ruffs the third spade with the ♦10. The ♦Q is cashed and the bad news is discovered when Jeremy discards the ♥A! He believes in making signals which are loud and clear. Declarer switches to clubs, playing the ace and a low one. Jane, who has correctly discarded the ♣2 earlier, has to win with the king and exit with a heart. Declarer ruffs, and plays ♦J8 and the ♣Q. Jane ruffs but declarer must still make his ♦3 and goes four down, losing 700. As his team mates are sitting East–West in Room 1 and also concede a penalty of 50 there is no balm in Gilead.

Once again a chukka ends and new partnerships are formed.

Rixi Markus discusses with her partner Zia Mahmood what went wrong, while Jeremy Flint, playing with Omar Sharif, studies his cards.

Co-presenters Sammy Kehela and Nicola Gardener relax while the cameras are repositioned for an interview.

Zia Mahmood (left) looks unhappy with his last result while Omar Sharif discusses strategy with his partner Jeremy Flint.

Robert Sheehan contemplates his next bid playing with Martin Hoffman. Jane Priday (left) and Irving Rose will defend this hand.

Zia Mahmood (centre) cracks a joke to relieve the pressure, much to the amusement of Martin Hoffman (left) and Irving Rose.

Omar Sharif checks the percentages before playing to the next trick.
Rixi Markus (right) considers the defence.

```
                    ♠ A 8
                    ♥ A 9 6 3
                    ◆ K 7 5 4
                    ♣ J 7 2
    ♠ 6 4            N          ♠ 9 5 3 2
    ♥ 8 2                       ♥ 10 7 5 4
    ◆ Q J 10 6 2  W    E        ◆ A 9 8 3
    ♣ Q 10 6 5       S          ♣ 8
                    ♠ K Q J 10 7
                    ♥ K Q J
                    ◆ —
                    ♣ A K 9 4 3
```

Possible auction

South	West	North	East
—	—	—	Pass
2♠	Pass	3◆	Pass
4♣	Pass	4♥	Pass
5♣	Pass	6♣	All pass

6 C is clearly the best contract depending on little more than a 3–2 trump break (a 68% chance). A 4–1 break is not necessarily insuperable but calls for extreme care in the play.

The ◆ Q is led so declarer ruffs and cashes the ♣ A K. When West shows up with four trumps to the queen ten it is necessary to effect an endplay. Deep analysis reveals that the contract cannot succeed unless West has at least two cards in each major suit. Furthermore South's remaining trumps are one too many. Declarer therefore crosses to dummy with the ♥ A and ruffs a diamond. The ♥ K is cashed and then spades are played. West is helpless; if he ruffs low, dummy overruns and a heart led to regain entry to the South hand which is high except for West's ♣ Q. If West ruffs with the ♣ Q and returns a diamond, declarer ruffs and continues spades and then the ♥ Q picking up West's ♣ 10 in the process. Finally if West ruffs with the ♣ Q and returns the ♣ 10 dummy wins but the carefully preserved low heart is the entry to declarer's hand and the established spades.

This is a difficult hand to play and requires expert technique. Any slight variation such as not ruffing a second diamond, or neglecting to cash two hearts early will result in defeat because trump control will be surrendered to West.

TIP When declarer needs a certain distribution for the success of a contract, he must play for it.

```
                    ♠ A 8
                    ♥ A 9 6 3
                    ♦ K 7 5 4
                    ♣ J 7 2
    ♠ 6 4              N           ♠ 9 5 3 2
    ♥ 8 2                          ♥ 10 7 5 4
    ♦ Q J 10 6 2    W     E        ♦ A 9 8 3
    ♣ Q 10 6 5         S           ♣ 8
                    ♠ K Q J 10 7
                    ♥ K Q J
                    ♦ —
                    ♣ A K 9 4 3
```

South	West	North	East
Zia Mahmood	*Omar Sharif*	*Rixi Markus*	*Jeremy Flint*
—	—	—	Pass
1♣	Pass	1♥	Pass
2♠	Pass	3 NT	Pass
4♦	Pass	4♠	Pass
4 NT	Pass	5♥	Pass
6♠	Pass	Pass	Pass

Ugh! It is usually a mistake for both partners to leap about during
the auction. Once South creates a forcing-to-game situation, North
should simply bid 2 NT. This leaves South more room to describe his
hand further by rebidding 3 S showing 5–5 or perhaps 6–5 in the
black suits. As it went South had a very difficult problem over 3 NT
and 4 D seems the best action but perhaps over 4 S, 5 C is better than
4 NT. Blackwood is rarely correct when holding a void.

The ♦ Q is led and declarer is soon in dire trouble. He tries for a
3–3 trump break which would give him more latitude. When that
fails his best chance is to drop the ♣ Q doubleton. It is not his lucky
day and he concedes 100 for going two down, and by the rules of the
competition he cannot even claim his 100 for honours in spades.

```
                    ♠ A 8
                    ♥ A 9 6 3
                    ♦ K 7 5 4
                    ♣ J 7 2
    ♠ 6 4               N           ♠ 9 5 3 2
    ♥ 8 2                           ♥ 10 7 5 4
    ♦ Q J 10 6 2   W       E        ♦ A 9 8 3
    ♣ Q 10 6 5          S           ♣ 8
                    ♠ K Q J 10 7
                    ♥ K Q J
                    ♦ —
                    ♣ A K 9 4 3
```

South	West	North	East
Martin Hoffman	*Irving Rose*	*Rob Sheehan*	*Jane Priday*
—	—	—	Pass
1♣	Pass	1♦	Pass
2♠	Pass	3♣	Pass
3♠	Pass	4♥	Pass
5♦	Pass	6♣	All pass

This was an excellent bidding sequence which owed much to Rob Sheehan's simple preference bid of 3 C. South's 3 S showed that he was 5–5 or 6–5 in the black suits and North cue bid the ♥ A. South showed his diamond control and North sensibly returned to his longer black suit at the six level.

Again I sit back about to enjoy, I hope, the sight of brilliant declarer play. West kills my hopes by the fanciful lead of the ♥ 2! What has come over him? I can see what he is trying to do. With four trumps to the queen, ten he wants declarer to think that he has a singleton heart and is trying for a ruff. Should declarer fall for the sucker punch and therefore cash the ♣ AK he will be defeated. Instead declarer wins, cashes the ♣ A, and leads a low club towards the jack. There is no further problem and he quickly wraps up twelve tricks, scoring 920.

Note the standard safety play of AK943 opposite J72 – Ace and low to the jack. If either hand shows out on the second round declarer is in control – the same play applies to AK94 opposite J652.

A swing of 1020 is the largest yet on any one board.

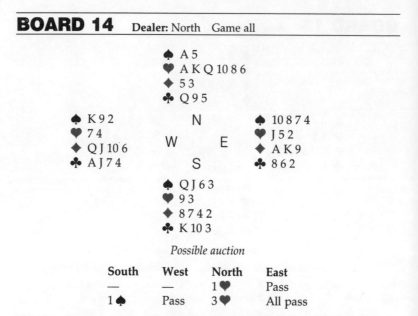

♠ A 5
♥ A K Q 10 8 6
♦ 5 3
♣ Q 9 5

♠ K 9 2   N   ♠ 10 8 7 4
♥ 7 4   W   E   ♥ J 5 2
♦ Q J 10 6   S   ♦ A K 9
♣ A J 7 4   ♣ 8 6 2

♠ Q J 6 3
♥ 9 3
♦ 8 7 4 2
♣ K 10 3

Possible auction

South	West	North	East
—	—	1♥	Pass
1♠	Pass	3♥	All pass

North has approximately seven playing tricks in a heart contract. This is shown by opening with 1 H and then jumping to 3 H on the next round. With eight playing tricks the opening bid would be 2 H. South has nothing in hand apart from his initial spade response and will not accept North's game try.

The defenders will play diamonds and declarer ruff the third round and draw trumps. Declarer sees that the uneasy contract can be made if East has the ♣ J because two club tricks can be assured by finessing the ten. Alternatively nine tricks are possible if West has the ♠ K, provided that declarer could be certain of gaining entry to dummy. Can these two lines of play be combined? The answer is 'Yes'.

Declarer leads the ♣ 9 and runs it. He sees that he can afford to lose a trick to West's ♣ J if the ♠ K is favourably placed. West is helpless and forced to take the ♣ J. When declarer regains the lead the ♣ Q is led and overtaken by dummy's king and a certain club entry to dummy is created. In due course dummy is entered with the ♣ 10 and the ♠ Q successfully finessed. If declarer makes the mistake of leading the ♣ Q and not the ♣ 9, West ducks. This not only kills dummy's club entry but protects West's ♠ K from attack. The contract can still be made if declarer then cashes the remaining two trumps because West is caught in a classical strip-squeeze ending, but declarer will still have to guess which are his last four cards, and play accordingly.

TIP Consider ducking the first round of a suit to force an entry to the hand opposite.

```
                    ♠ A 5
                    ♥ A K Q 10 8 6
                    ♦ 5 3
                    ♣ Q 9 5
    ♠ K 9 2          N              ♠ 10 8 7 4
    ♥ 7 4                           ♥ J 5 2
    ♦ Q J 10 6    W     E           ♦ A K 9
    ♣ A J 7 4        S              ♣ 8 6 2
                    ♠ Q J 6 3
                    ♥ 9 3
                    ♦ 8 7 4 2
                    ♣ K 10 3
```

South	West	North	East
Zia Mahmood	*Omar Sharif*	*Rixi Markus*	*Jeremy Flint*
—	—	1♥	Pass
1♠	Pass	3♥	All pass

My bidding, or theirs, is improving!

The ♦ A is led and Omar Sharif, West, plays the queen. This is a signal which guarantees the ♦ J. East continues with the ♦ K and Omar plays the six. The ♦ 9 follows and Omar plays the ten. Normally in this type of situation a defender plays the card he is known to hold. By playing the ♦ J West cannot fool his partner, only declarer, but Omar has a deep laid plot afoot. The declarer, Rixi Markus, cashes the ♥ AKQ and Omar gently discards the ♣ 4. Now look at the position from declarer's viewpoint.

Rixi knows that Omar has the ♦ J. If therefore East has the ♠ K the contract must succeed and there is still a 50 per cent chance of making her ninth trick even if Omar has the ♠ K. Rixi therefore cashes the ♠ A and leads another. Omar wins and leads the ♦ J. Rixi ruffs and leads the ♣ Q but Omar, with a smile, declines the apple, and instead accepts 100 for holding declarer to eight tricks.

```
                        ♠ A 5
                        ♥ A K Q 10 8 6
                        ♦ 5 3
                        ♣ Q 9 5
        ♠ K 9 2          N          ♠ 10 8 7 4
        ♥ 7 4                        ♥ J 5 2
        ♦ Q J 10 6    W     E        ♦ A K 9
        ♣ A J 7 4        S           ♣ 8 6 2
                        ♠ Q J 6 3
                        ♥ 9 3
                        ♦ 8 7 4 2
                        ♣ K 10 3
```

South	West	North	East
Martin Hoffman	*Irving Rose*	*Rob Sheehan*	*Jane Priday*
—	—	1 ♥	Pass
1 ♠	Pass	3 ♥	All pass

No comment!

The ♦A is led. Irving Rose, West, signals with the ♦Q. The ♦K is cashed and Irving plays the six. On the ♦9 he false-cards by playing the ♦J. Rob Sheehan, declarer, ruffs and considers the problem. The missing diamond is the ten and it could be in either hand. There is no point in brooding over it so Rob plays the ♥AKQ and Irving discards the ♣4. The ♣Q comes next but East follows with the two and Irving with the seven. Rob abandons the club suit and cashes the ♥10 and the ♥8. This intriguing end position arises:

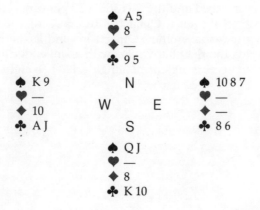

```
                        ♠ A 5
                        ♥ 8
                        ♦ —
                        ♣ 9 5
        ♠ K 9            N          ♠ 10 8 7
        ♥ —                          ♥ —
        ♦ 10          W     E        ♦ —
        ♣ A J            S           ♣ 8 6
                        ♠ Q J
                        ♥ —
                        ♦ 8
                        ♣ K 10
```

On the ♥8, East discards the ♣6, dummy the ♦8, and Irving the
♠9. If Rob now leads a club Irving will win and cash the ♦10 and
another club to defeat the contract. Rob, however, has seen Irving
before and is well aware of how he behaves in a strip-squeeze situation, so he places the ♠A on the table! Well played Rob.

BOARD 15   Dealer: West   East–West vulnerable

```
                    ♠ J 10 9
                    ♥ K 10 9 7
                    ♦ Q 7 2
                    ♣ 10 4 3
      ♠ K 5              N              ♠ A 7 2
      ♥ A J 8 5 3                       ♥ Q 6 4 2
      ♦ A J 6       W        E          ♦ K 5
      ♣ 8 6 2                           ♣ A K Q 5
                        S
                    ♠ Q 8 6 4 3
                    ♥ —
                    ♦ 10 9 8 4 3
                    ♣ J 9 7
```

Possible auction

South	West	North	East
—	1 ♥	Pass	3 ♣
Pass	3 ♥	Pass	4 NT
Pass	5 ♥	Pass	6 ♥
Pass	Pass	Pass	

When West opens the bidding with 1 H, East must force to game
and 3 C is a good choice. The alternative, which participants in this
tournament are not permitted to use, is to call 2 NT. This is a conventional bid called Baron, named after its inventor, Leo Baron, which
indicates a balanced hand with at least sixteen points. Its adherents
claim that its main advantage is in a negative sense. When responder forces in a suit he guarantees a good five-card suit.

Against the heart slam, North leads the ♠J. Declarer wins in
hand and sees that twelve tricks are almost certain provided that the
trumps are not 4–0. The ♥3 should be led so that if North shows
out, dummy's queen can be played. By leading twice from dummy
it is then possible to pick up South's trumps without further loss.

On this occasion the ♥Q wins and South shows out. The contract
can then only be made by stripping North of his exit cards in the

side suits. Then he will have to win trick eleven with a trump and suicidally return a trump at trick twelve. Declarer has to hope that North's hand is shaped 3–4–3–3, 2–4–3–4 or 3–4–2–4. The common factor, apart from the four trumps, in these hand patterns is that there are at least three clubs. It is this suit which declarer therefore plays first. When he discovers that it breaks evenly he has to rely on North having a 3–4–3–3 shape. Accordingly he cashes the ♦ K and ♦ A and ruffs the ♦ J. Then comes the ♠ A and a spade ruff. The end position has arrived, so declarer leads the ♥ 8 and North capitulates.

TIP Anticipate that the trump suit breaks badly and plan accordingly.

BOARD 15   Dealer: West   East–West vulnerable   Room 1

	♠ J 10 9	
	♥ K 10 9 7	
	♦ Q 7 2	
	♣ 10 4 3	

♠ K 5		♠ A 7 2
♥ A J 8 5 3	N	♥ Q 6 4 2
♦ A J 6	W E	♦ K 5
♣ 8 6 2	S	♣ A K Q 5

	♠ Q 8 6 4 3	
	♥ —	
	♦ 10 9 8 4 3	
	♣ J 9 7	

South	West	North	East
Zia Mahmood	Omar Sharif	Rixi Markus	Jeremy Flint
—	1♥	Pass	3♣
3 NT	Pass	Pass	6♥
Pass	Pass	Pass	

The auction took a surprising turn when Zia Mahmood bid 3 NT. I thought at first I had misheard because that was the alternative rebid to 3 H which I thought dealer might make. Zia had merely introduced a conventional bid into the auction. His call was an example of the so-called Unusual No Trump (UNT for short). It indicated at least five cards in both the unbid suits and, at the favourable vulnerability, suggested a sacrifice to his partner. When West passed so did North. Rixi Markus was quite prepared for Zia to go umpteen down undoubled in 3 NT. Jeremy Flint, however, brushed them both aside by bidding 6 H.

The ♠ J is led. Declarer wins in hand and not appreciating that he may be able to overcome a 4–0 trump split in either hand, places the ♥ A on the table. From this moment his contract has no chance and he soon concedes 100.

BOARD 15   **Dealer:** West   East–West vulnerable   ## Room 2

```
                    ♠ J 10 9
                    ♥ K 10 9 7
                    ♦ Q 7 2
                    ♣ 10 4 3
  ♠ K 5              N            ♠ A 7 2
  ♥ A J 8 5 3                     ♥ Q 6 4 2
  ♦ A J 6       W       E         ♦ K 5
  ♣ 8 6 2            S            ♣ A K Q 5
                    ♠ Q 8 6 4 3
                    ♥ —
                    ♦ 10 9 8 4 3
                    ♣ J 9 7
```

South	West	North	East
Martin Hoffman	Irving Rose	Rob Sheehan	Jane Priday
—	1♥	Pass	3♣
Pass	3 NT	Pass	4♥
Pass	4 NT	Pass	5♥
Pass	6♥	All pass	

The auction was fairly routine. West chose to bid 3 NT instead of 3 H, the rebid which I prefer, but there is little in it. West is full value for his subsequent bidding; he has a diamond and a spade control, also a fifth heart tucked away.

The ♠ J is led. Declarer plays dummy's ace and leads the ♥ Q. When South shows out there is no chance of making the contract. Declarer will thank his lucky stars that the board is tied, but it is a missed opportunity.

Declarer played too quickly. He saw that he could pick up four trumps with South if he made the safety play of leading the ♥ Q. What he should have foreseen is that it costs him nothing to lose the first trick to South with the ♥ K. The advantage is that given a favourable distribution of the other suits he may be able to effect an endplay in trumps, should North hold all four missing hearts. It is then quite clear that the first trick should be won in hand and a low heart led to the queen.

BOARD 16   Dealer: South   North–South vulnerable

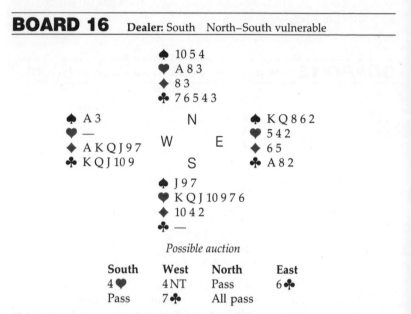

♠ 10 5 4
♥ A 8 3
♦ 8 3
♣ 7 6 5 4 3

♠ A 3
♥ —
♦ A K Q J 9 7
♣ K Q J 10 9

♠ K Q 8 6 2
♥ 5 4 2
♦ 6 5
♣ A 8 2

♠ J 9 7
♥ K Q J 10 9 7 6
♦ 10 4 2
♣ —

Possible auction

South	West	North	East
4♥	4NT	Pass	6♣
Pass	7♣	All pass	

This is an interesting bidding hand and East–West would do very well indeed to reach 7 C after South's pre-emptive bid of 4 H. West has two possible courses of action. A bid of 4 NT must be minor suit orientated because it bypasses spades. East has good cards especially the ♣ A and he should jump to 6 C. If his partner, at the favourable vulnerability, really is looking for a sacrifice, no great harm is done because the opponents would be bound to push on to 5 H. When, however, West has a giant two-suiter the jump bid may encourage him to bid the grand slam.

The other possible course of action for West is to bid 5 H committing his side to a small slam at least. The danger is that East will bid 6 S and West will have to remove to 7 C or 7 D. If he chooses the latter, South should double for an unusual lead. It will not take North long to realize that a club is required. West, of course, should not blindly bid 7 D but instead consult his partner further by bidding 6 NT over 6 S and then East will call 7 C.

Another noteworthy feature in this type of auction is North's action. Usually he does best by passing because he should realize that he has no defence and the opponents have not yet bid a slam.

A contract of 7 C may appear to be hazardous after a heart lead because of the 5–0 trump split. This is not so because once the bad break is discovered, declarer cashes the ♠ A and then runs diamonds until North ruffs. He then overruffs and draws trumps. The ♠ A has to be cashed first to prevent North from discarding the suit and then ruffing the ♠ A when it is played.

TIP When trumps are not drawn, cash essential side suit winners before the defenders discard their cards in those suits.

BOARD 16 **Dealer:** South   North–South vulnerable Room 1

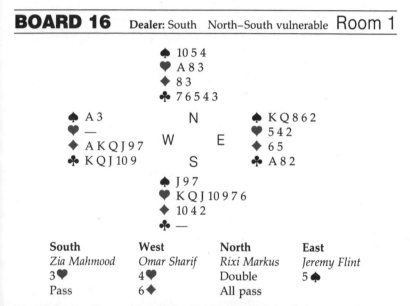

South	West	North	East
Zia Mahmood	*Omar Sharif*	*Rixi Markus*	*Jeremy Flint*
3♥	4♥	Double	5♠
Pass	6♦	All pass	

Zia Mahmood's opening bid of 3 H is academically correct. Even if his partner can supply but one trick he will only go down 500 if doubled, but then his opponents will almost certainly have a slam on with their cards. The disadvantage of 3 H is that South has a void and I do not like to pre-empt at the three level with a first round control outside the long trump suit. Omar Sharif's cue bid of 4 H shows a giant two-suiter. Rixi Markus doubles to show heart support but I prefer to pass in such situations to avoid increasing East's options. He can pass with a poor hand in the knowledge that his partner gets another chance; he can bid, and thereby show values, or he can redouble, to show general all-round strength. With Jeremy Flint's hand I think 5 S is the value bid and sounds forcing to a slam in spades or in a minor. When Omar in fact retreats to 6 D I suspect that both partners were a little uneasy. Luckily they did not reach 7 D because Zia would have made a Lightner slam double. This is a convention invented by the late Theodore Lightner of the USA where a double of a slam requests partner to find an unusual lead normally because the doubler is void in a suit.

Even without the double, Rixi's nose is working overtime because she leads the ♣ 7! Zia ruffs and returns a heart but declarer ruffs and draws trumps, scoring 920 (120 + 300 not vulnerable + 500 small slam bonus, honours not counting).

BOARD 16   Dealer: South   North–South vulnerable   Room 2

```
                    ♠ 10 5 4
                    ♥ A 8 3
                    ♦ 8 3
                    ♣ 7 6 5 4 3
    ♠ A 3                N              ♠ K Q 8 6 2
    ♥ —                                 ♥ 5 4 2
    ♦ A K Q J 9 7     W     E           ♦ 6 5
    ♣ K Q J 10 9         S              ♣ A 8 2
                    ♠ J 9 7
                    ♥ K Q J 10 9 7 6
                    ♦ 10 4 2
                    ♣ —
```

South	West	North	East
Martin Hoffman	*Irving Rose*	*Rob Sheehan*	*Jane Priday*
3♥	4♥	Pass	6♠
Pass	7♣	All pass	

Again a South player values his hand as worth only a three level pre-emptive bid because he is vulnerable. Note that Rob Sheehan passes 4 H which is what I recommended. East's jump to 6 S is a little wild. Certainly there are the values for a bid at the six level but there is a doubt about the suit. If partner has spades it would be very easy to miss a grand slam, and if he has the minor suits he may be too high in seven. Perhaps a bid of 5 H, passing the buck back to partner is the best action. It is certainly very difficult.

As it went Irving Rose made a master bid with the West cards. His call of 7 C denied spades and hence implied diamonds as well as clubs. Holding more clubs than diamonds his partner therefore passed.

The ♥A is led. Irving ruffs and cashes the ♣J. When South discards the ♥7 Irving scarcely pauses. He merely counts up the number of discards he can obtain on his diamond suit. The answer is four.

Accordingly he cashes one top spade before running his diamonds. When North ruffs he is overruffed and trumps are drawn and thirteen tricks claimed.

It is the mark of an expert technician merely to cash one round of spades. The bidding has made the possibility of North having a singleton spade remote, but Irving's play is undoubtedly correct. If no spade is cashed before the fifth diamond is played, North will discard all his spades, and this will be the end position:

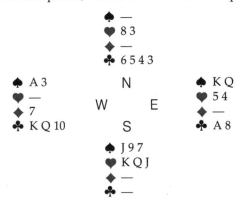

```
              ♠ —
              ♥ 8 3
              ♦ —
              ♣ 6 5 4 3
  ♠ A 3          N          ♠ K Q
  ♥ —                       ♥ 5 4
  ♦ 7        W     E        ♦ —
  ♣ K Q 10       S          ♣ A 8
              ♠ J 9 7
              ♥ K Q J
              ♦ —
              ♣ —
```

On the ♦7 North discards a heart and dummy a spade. Declarer must then play a spade which North ruffs and defeats the contract. That is why declarer projects the play to this point and sees in advance the necessity for cashing one top spade while it is safe to do so.

For making 7 C, Irving scores 1440 (140 + 300 not vulnerable game + 1000 grand slam bonus but no honours). The net difference is therefore 520 to East–West in Room 2 and North–South in Room 1.

On this note it is time to change partners again, but we are past halfway.

```
                      ♠ Q 8 6 2
                      ♥ J 8 7
                      ♦ J 3
                      ♣ Q J 10 8
     ♠ 5 4              N            ♠ A K
     ♥ 6 2                           ♥ A K 10 3
     ♦ A Q 10 9 6 2   W     E        ♦ 8 5
     ♣ 9 5 3            S            ♣ A 7 6 4 2
                      ♠ J 10 9 7 3
                      ♥ Q 9 5 4
                      ♦ K 7 4
                      ♣ K
```

Possible auction

South	West	North	East
—	—	Pass	1♣
Pass	1♦	Pass	2♥
Pass	3♦	Pass	3NT
Pass	Pass	Pass	

The ♠ J is led. Declarer sees that his only chance is to make at least four tricks in diamonds, but dummy has no outside entry. With this diamond combination the correct technique is to finesse first the ♦ 8 and subsequently the ♦ 9. Whenever the suit breaks 3–2 and South has one of the honour cards five tricks materialize.

When experts meet, however, all is not sweetness and light. North will appreciate declarer's dilemma and allow the ♦ 8 to hold the trick. Subsequently when the ♦ 5 is led and South contributes the seven declarer will realize that North may be trying to deceive him. If South started with ♦ KJ74 there is nothing to be done; he must go off. Accordingly he must play North to hold originally, either the ♦ J3 or the ♦ K3, but which? There is but one straw in the wind. South, too, is an expert and with ♦ J73 originally he might have played the ♦ J on the second round to muddy the waters further. Is this a clue or a double bluff? We shall have to wait and see.

TIP For defenders: duck an honour smoothly when sitting over an otherwise entryless dummy containing a long suit, to give declarer problems.

```
                    ♠ Q 8 6 2
                    ♥ J 8 7
                    ♦ J 3
                    ♣ Q J 10 8
      ♠ 5 4              N              ♠ A K
      ♥ 6 2                             ♥ A K 10 3
      ♦ A Q 10 9 6 2  W     E           ♦ 8 5
      ♣ 9 5 3              S            ♣ A 7 6 4 2
                    ♠ J 10 9 7 3
                    ♥ Q 9 5 4
                    ♦ K 7 4
                    ♣ K
```

South	West	North	East
Omar Sharif	*Martin Hoffman*	*Rixi Markus*	*Jane Priday*
—	—	Pass	1 ♣
Pass	1 ♦	Pass	1 ♥
Pass	2 ♦	Pass	2 NT
Pass	Pass	Pass	

A conservative auction but not the best part-score contract. 3 D is virtually 'throw at the wall'.

The ♠ J is led. Jane Priday wins and introduces a new twist by leading the ♣ 2. If the clubs break 3–2 (a 68% chance) this is the best hope of success. Omar Sharif plays the king and Rixi Markus signals violently with the queen. In my view this is a mistake because it may warn declarer off playing a second round of clubs. Jane, however, is not put off and after winning the ♠ 10 return, not only cashes the ♣ A but continues with a club when South shows out discarding the ♥ 5. Rixi wins and, instead of cashing the ♠ Q as expected, plays the ♥ 8. Declarer wins and leads another club. South, confused by his partner's defence, does not want to discard a red card, and disastrously parts with the ♠ 3. Declarer, with the aid of the diamond finesse, therefore makes eight tricks for a score of 120. Heigh-ho!

```
                    ♠ Q 8 6 2
                    ♥ J 8 7
                    ♦ J 3
                    ♣ Q J 10 8
    ♠ 5 4              N            ♠ A K
    ♥ 6 2                           ♥ A K 10 3
    ♦ A Q 10 9 6 2   W    E         ♦ 8 5
    ♣ 9 5 3            S            ♣ A 7 6 4 2
                    ♠ J 10 9 7 3
                    ♥ Q 9 5 4
                    ♦ K 7 4
                    ♣ K
```

South	West	North	East
Jeremy Flint	*Rob Sheehan*	*Zia Mahmood*	*Irving Rose*
—	—	Pass	1 ♣
1 ♠	Pass	2 ♠	Double
Pass	4 ♦	All pass	

Jeremy Flint's enterprise in overcalling 1 S made life difficult for the opponents but Irving Rose (East) doubled to force his partner to bid. When there is no good bid available, you sometimes have to compromise and make the best available bid. In this case, double has the merit of suggesting a good hand with spade shortage. Rob Sheehan had visions of a possible 5 D contract when he leapt encouragingly to 4 D – but there the auction rightly closed.

There is no problem in the play, Rob simply finesses first the ♦10, and, when this is unsuccessful, tries the nine, which brings in ten tricks for 130 points. So the net difference is 10 points – a washout.

```
                    ♠ J 10
                    ♥ A J
                    ♦ K 8 6 5 2
                    ♣ A J 6 4
        ♠ 9 7 4 2         N          ♠ 8 5 3
        ♥ 10 9 8 3                   ♥ Q 6 5 4 2
        ♦ J 9 7 4     W       E      ♦ 10
        ♣ 8               S          ♣ K 10 9 2
                    ♠ A K Q 6
                    ♥ K 7
                    ♦ A Q 3
                    ♣ Q 7 5 3
```

Possible auction

South	West	North	East
2 NT	Pass	6 NT	Pass
Pass	Pass		

Contracts of 6 C or 6 D are unlucky to be defeated but 6 NT is clearly superior.

The ♥ 10 is led. Declarer wins and cashes the ♦ A, the ♣ A and then the ♦ Q, learning the bad news. It is time to use the second string to declarer's bow by playing clubs for three tricks. There is an elegant sure trick solution. He merely leads the ♠ 6 to the jack and returns the ♣ 4 to his queen. East must duck because he cannot allow the ♣ K to 'beat air'. When declarer has his second club trick safely in the bank he changes tack and leads the ♦ 3 to the king and returns a diamond, setting up his twelfth trick in the suit.

But what if West has four clubs and wins the queen with the king? He can then return the ♦ J setting up his nine. Although declarer has only eleven top tricks West cannot protect both minor suits and he succumbs to a squeeze. Declarer plays off the ♥ A and three rounds of spades, leaving this end position:

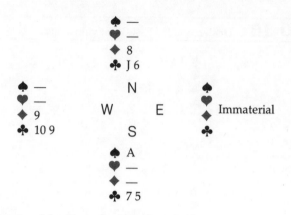

```
            ♠ —
            ♥ —
            ♦ 8
            ♣ J 6
  ♠ —          N          ♠
  ♥ —                     ♥  Immaterial
  ♦ 9      W     E        ♦
  ♣ 10 9        S         ♣
            ♠ A
            ♥ —
            ♦ —
            ♣ 7 5
```

He cannot safely discard on declarer's ♠ A.

TIP When your contract is probable, look for a certainty.

BOARD 18   Dealer: South   East–West vulnerable   Room 1

```
                    ♠ J 10
                    ♥ A J
                    ♦ K 8 6 5 2
                    ♣ A J 6 4
  ♠ 9 7 4 2            N          ♠ 8 5 3
  ♥ 10 9 8 3                      ♥ Q 6 5 4 2
  ♦ J 9 7 4      W        E       ♦ 10
  ♣ 8                  S          ♣ K 10 9 2
                    ♠ A K Q 6
                    ♥ K 7
                    ♦ A Q 3
                    ♣ Q 7 5 3
```

South	West	North	East
Omar Sharif	*Martin Hoffman*	*Rixi Markus*	*Jane Priday*
2 NT	Pass	6 NT	Pass
Pass	Pass		

No problem with the auction or the final contract.

The ♥ 10 is led. Dummy's jack is played, and East's queen is won in hand. A club is played to the ace and the four returned to the queen. There is no point in Jane Priday playing her king because that would have surrendered three club tricks. When declarer's queen wins and West shows out there is obviously no future in playing another club. Instead Omar Sharif cashes the ♦ A Q and when East discards the ♥ 2 it is easy for declarer to play a third round of diamonds to the king and return a diamond to West's jack. This effectively sets up dummy's ♦ 8 as the twelfth trick.

For making his small slam Omar earned 990 points. I consulted my friend Derek Rimington on this hand, and he made the following observation.

Say the layout of the hand had been different:

```
                  ♠ J 10
                  ♥ A J
                  ♦ K 8 6 5 2
                  ♣ A J 6 4
   ♠ 9 7 4 2           N          ♠ 8 5 3
   ♥ 10 9 8 3                      ♥ Q 6 5 4 2
   ♦ 10          W       E        ♦ J 9 7 4
   ♣ K 10 9 8                      ♣ 2
                      S
                  ♠ A K Q 6
                  ♥ K 7
                  ♦ A Q 3
                  ♣ Q 7 5 3
```

The lead would be the same and when declarer plays the ♣ 3, West still plays the eight. Dummy's ace wins but when the ♣ 4 is led, East shows out and the contract is unmakeable. West wins declarer's queen with the king and plays any card at random. It matters not, one of the defenders must make one more trick in a minor suit.

If, however, the correct method of playing on diamonds first is adopted the contract succeeds on the actual hand and also on the one set out above. Let us play through the latter. The ♦ A is cashed and when both opponents follow it is safe to cross to dummy with the ♣ A in case East has the ♣ K singleton. Then a diamond is led to the queen, and West shows out. It is time to switch back to clubs.

The technique is simply to lead a low club through the hand which is short in diamonds, in this case West. So the ♣ 3 is led and West cannot afford to play his king so dummy's jack wins. When East discards, declarer switches back to diamonds and safely sets up his twelfth trick.

```
                    ♠ J 10
                    ♥ A J
                    ♦ K 8 6 5 2
                    ♣ A J 6 4
      ♠ 9 7 4 2         N          ♠ 8 5 3
      ♥ 10 9 8 3                    ♥ Q 6 5 4 2
      ♦ J 9 7 4    W       E        ♦ 10
      ♣ 8              S            ♣ K 10 9 2
                    ♠ A K Q 6
                    ♥ K 7
                    ♦ A Q 3
                    ♣ Q 7 5 3
```

South	West	North	East
Jeremy Flint	*Rob Sheehan*	*Zia Mahmood*	*Irving Rose*
2 NT	Pass	3 ♣	Pass
3 ♠	Pass	6 NT	All pass

Presumably North–South were using the Baron convention whereby a response of 3 C requests the opener to bid his suits upwards. Thus the 3 S rebid denied four diamonds and four hearts but guaranteed a four-card spade suit. North had heard enough, and elected to play in 6 NT. Presumably if South had rebid 3 D indicating four of them, or 3 NT showing a club suit, North might have tried for a grand slam. His partner would need to hold precise cards, something like:

```
      ♠ A K 3 2              ♠ A K 3
      ♥ K 7 2         or     ♥ K 7 2
      ♦ A Q J 3              ♦ A Q 3
      ♣ K 3                  ♣ K Q 5 3
```

but it costs nothing to try.

In 6 NT Jeremy Flint soon demonstrates almost the best technical way of playing the hand. The ♥ 10 is led and the jack, queen and king are played in that order. Then the ♦ A Q are cashed and East shows out on trick three discarding the ♥ 4. Jeremy immediately switches to clubs by leading the three and playing dummy's ace. The ♣ 4 is led back through East who follows with the nine. Jeremy wins the queen and concedes a diamond to West.

He will not be surprised to find that the board is a washout. As the cards lie it is virtually impossible for a good player to fail to make 6 NT. He will, however, no doubt be aggrieved to find that his extra precaution in playing on diamonds first goes unrewarded.

```
                    ♠ J 8 2
                    ♥ K 5
                    ♦ A 8 2
                    ♣ Q J 10 7 2
      ♠ 5 4            N          ♠ 9 7 3
      ♥ Q 10 6 3                  ♥ A 9 7
      ♦ 9 7 5 4 3    W     E      ♦ Q 10 6
      ♣ 9 8            S          ♣ A K 4 3
                    ♠ A K Q 10 6
                    ♥ J 8 4 2
                    ♦ K J
                    ♣ 6 5
```

Possible auction

South	West	North	East
—	—	—	1 NT
Double	2♦	Pass	Pass
2♠	Pass	4♠	All pass

Modern bidding practice is to regard North's pass as forcing; South must bid again. Against 4 S a club lead to the king, followed by the ♣ A and a third club will force declarer to ruff high. East for his opening bid of 1 NT must have precisely thirteen high card points which leaves West with one of the red queens at most. Declarer must hope that East has the ♦ Q but he still lacks entries to finesse the ♦ J, cash the ♦ K and return to dummy to cash the ♦ A. One chance would appear to be to lead the ♠ 6 and finesse the ♠ 8 hoping that West has the nine. Quite plausible but it will not work against an expert because the ♠ 9 will be played on the ♠ 6 thus blocking the trump suit. A second chance is to play West to hold the doubleton ♠ 9. The ♠ A is cashed, then the ♠ 10 led but declarer is unlucky because the ♠ 9 does not appear. The ♠ 10 is allowed to hold the trick and the ♠ 6 is then led to dummy's jack. The ♣ Q J are cashed and two losing hearts discarded. The ♦ J is then finessed. The ♠ Q is played and both opponents are squeezed. This is the end position:

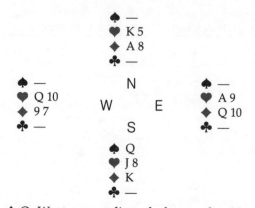

```
            ♠ —
            ♥ K 5
            ♦ A 8
            ♣ —
    ♠ —          N          ♠ —
    ♥ Q 10              W   E      ♥ A 9
    ♦ 9 7                          ♦ Q 10
    ♣ —          S          ♣ —
            ♠ Q
            ♥ J 8
            ♦ K
            ♣ —
```

On the ♠ Q, West cannot discard a heart otherwise declarer throws dummy's ♦ 8 and leads a heart making the last two tricks. West therefore has to discard a diamond. Dummy's ♥ 5 is discarded, its useful life is over, and East is under pressure. He cannot throw a diamond because dummy's ace, eight would both make. If he discards the ♥ 9, declarer cashes the ♦ K and exits with a heart. East will then bridge the gap to dummy!

TIP Keep a sharp look out for a hidden entry.

BOARD 19   **Dealer:** East   North–South vulnerable   Room 1

```
                    ♠ J 8 2
                    ♥ K 5
                    ♦ A 8 2
                    ♣ Q J 10 7 2
    ♠ 5 4              N          ♠ 9 7 3
    ♥ Q 10 6 3                    ♥ A 9 7
    ♦ 9 7 5 4 3     W   E         ♦ Q 10 6
    ♣ 9 8              S          ♣ A K 4 3
                    ♠ A K Q 10 6
                    ♥ J 8 4 2
                    ♦ K J
                    ♣ 6 5
```

South	West	North	East
Omar Sharif	*Martin Hoffman*	*Rixi Markus*	*Jane Priday*
—	—	—	1 NT
Pass	2 ♦	Pass	Pass
2 ♠	Pass	Pass	3 ♦
3 ♥	Pass	3 ♠	All pass

Again I am surprised by the auction. I would have thought that Omar Sharif could make a sporting double of East's weak no trump. Admittedly a double of a no trump is always for penalties and South would therefore like to be a little stronger, but he does have a good lead. There is a very real danger in passing, because so might West and North on their actual hands. West, however, runs to 2D although I would prefer to pass. South then comes to life but the damage has been done and the auction ends with a bid of 3S.

The ♣9 is led. Jane Priday wins with the king and sees that her only real chance of beating the part-score contract is to find her partner with the ♦K and perhaps a trump trick. She therefore attacks by returning the ♦6 but Omar's jack wins and there is no further difficulty for declarer in making ten tricks because the spot cards in clubs lie so favourably for him.

BOARD 19   Dealer: East   North–South vulnerable   Room 2

```
                    ♠ J 8 2
                    ♥ K 5
                    ♦ A 8 2
                    ♣ Q J 10 7 2
     ♠ 5 4              N            ♠ 9 7 3
     ♥ Q 10 6 3                      ♥ A 9 7
     ♦ 9 7 5 4 3     W     E         ♦ Q 10 6
     ♣ 9 8              S            ♣ A K 4 3
                    ♠ A K Q 10 6
                    ♥ J 8 4 2
                    ♦ K J
                    ♣ 6 5
```

South	West	North	East
Jeremy Flint	*Rob Sheehan*	*Zia Mahmood*	*Irving Rose*
—	—	—	1 NT
2 ♠	Pass	4 ♠	All pass

A better auction; Jeremy Flint refused to be shut out when vulnerable and overcalled. Zia Mahmood naturally went straight to game.

The ♣9 is led. Irving Rose wins with the king and inconsiderately ruins my set hand by returning the ♦Q. Declarer wins with the ♦K and expertly unblocks the ♦J. The ♠KQ are cashed and then a club is led. Jeremy is in full control; he can win any return, draw the outstanding trump with dummy's jack and perhaps make eleven tricks. Irving puts an end to his musing, by cashing the ♥ A effectively conceding ten tricks.

There is a considerable swing on this board: 620 less 170 = 450 to North–South in Room 2 and East–West in Room 1.

BOARD 20   **Dealer:** West   Game all

```
              ♠ Q 10 8 5 2
              ♥ A J 6
              ♦ 8
              ♣ Q 10 8 4

   ♠ K J 9        N        ♠ A 6
   ♥ Q 9 4 3               ♥ 10 2
   ♦ A Q 2    W     E      ♦ K 7 6 5 4
   ♣ 7 5 3        S        ♣ A K 6 2

              ♠ 7 4 3
              ♥ K 8 7 5
              ♦ J 10 9 3
              ♣ J 9
```

Possible auction

South	West	North	East
—	1 NT	Pass	3 NT
Pass	Pass	Pass	

The uninformative auction will not warn off North from leading the ♠ 5. This will give declarer a cheap trick with the ♠ 9. A non-expert player would simply cash the ♦ A Q and concede defeat when the suit breaks 4–1, because the ninth trick is the ♠ K but there is no entry and the opponents will not obligingly lead the suit.

A cunning player might see that there is a difficulty with the third round of spades. He might decide to return a spade at trick two to unblock the suit. The ♦ A Q are cashed but again the 4–1 break is troublesome. The ♠ K can be cashed but when South wins the fourth round of diamonds he simply leads a heart for North to win the jack and cash two spade tricks. There are still further losers in the heart suit resulting in a two-trick set.

The expert takes it all in his stride. He can see ten tricks if the diamonds break 3–2 and therefore he takes out insurance. At trick two he plays the ♦ A to test for a 5–0 diamond break. If both opponents follow the ♠ A is unblocked and a diamond ducked in both hands. The ♦ Q is the entry back to hand and the ♣ A K the entries to dummy to cash the remaining diamond winners.

TIP Visualize the bad breaks and if necessary duck a trick to maintain communication.

BOARD 20   **Dealer:** West Game all   **Room 1**

```
                  ♠ Q 10 8 5 2
                  ♥ A J 6
                  ♦ 8
                  ♣ Q 10 8 4
    ♠ K J 9            N            ♠ A 6
    ♥ Q 9 4 3                       ♥ 10 2
    ♦ A Q 2        W       E        ♦ K 7 6 5 4
    ♣ 7 5 3            S            ♣ A K 6 2
                  ♠ 7 4 3
                  ♥ K 8 7 5
                  ♦ J 10 9 3
                  ♣ J 9
```

South	West	North	East
Omar Sharif	*Martin Hoffman*	*Rixi Markus*	*Jane Priday*
—	1 NT	Pass	3 NT
Pass	Pass	Pass	

I cannot fault this bidding sequence.

The ♠ 5 is led. Martin Hoffman wins in hand with the jack, crosses to dummy with a spade to unblock and ducks a diamond to South's nine. This is a competent way to play the hand. My only criticism, and it is very minor, is that a high diamond should be cashed before ducking a diamond. Admittedly a 5–0 break is unlikely but it costs nothing to find out. If the diamonds are 5–0 the second string to declarer's bow is to find the club's 3–3 so he will then duck the first round of that suit instead.

```
                    ♠ Q 10 8 5 2
                    ♥ A J 6
                    ♦ 8
                    ♣ Q 10 8 4
     ♠ K J 9           N           ♠ A 6
     ♥ Q 9 4 3                      ♥ 10 2
     ♦ A Q 2      W       E         ♦ K 7 6 5 4
     ♣ 7 5 3           S           ♣ A K 6 2
                    ♠ 7 4 3
                    ♥ K 8 7 5
                    ♦ J 10 9 3
                    ♣ J 9
```

South	West	North	East
Jeremy Flint	*Rob Sheehan*	*Zia Mahmood*	*Irving Rose*
—	Pass	Pass	1♦
Pass	1♥	1♠	2♣
Pass	3NT	All pass	

Rob Sheehan, and who could really blame him at this vulnerability, decided against opening a weak no trump with the West hand. The best contract of 3NT was still reached but North was warned off leading a spade when his partner took no action following his intervention. Instead the ♣ 4 was led!

This is a killing lead; I wonder what Rob will do? Like greased lightning Rob wins in dummy and leads the ♥ 2 and plays the queen on South's eight, North ducks! I sympathize with North; it certainly looks as though declarer has the ♥ K Q. Naturally Rob abandons the heart suit and cashes the ♦ A and ducks a diamond to South's nine. The ♣ J is returned and dummy wins. The ♦ Q is unblocked and dummy re-entered with the ♠ A. Two more diamonds are cashed. North, still clinging to his preconceived idea that declarer started with the ♥ K Q, becomes pseudo squeezed and discards the ♣ Q and ♠ 10. (He has already parted with the ♠ 2 and ♠ 5 when the diamonds were played.) The spade six is led to the king and North's queen falls. Declarer continues by cashing the ♠ J for his tenth trick!

Instead of using the term pseudo squeeze, I think that I will invent a new term, 'persuado squeeze', to describe this deal. North, of course, realized that declarer could not possibly have all the missing honour cards because of his initial pass. His duck in diamonds

surely meant that he had the ♠ K and therefore not the ♥ K, or he
would have had to play for the maximum number of diamond
tricks. Reasoning of this type, however, is not easy after one has
been in the recording studio playing on and off, for over twelve
hours.

One clue, which North missed, is that Rob is noted for the
deliberate way in which he plays or defends. When he quickly led
the heart to the queen at trick two it was so uncharacteristic that it
was suspicious. The net swing on the board was, however, only 30
points but a good initial lead was wasted.

This ends the fifth set of four boards and partners change again.

BOARD 21   Dealer: North   North–South vulnerable

```
                    ♠ 8 5
                    ♥ J 9 6 5 4 2
                    ♦ J 9 2
                    ♣ 10 7

    ♠ Q 9 3            N           ♠ K 7 2
    ♥ Q 7 3                        ♥ A K 8
    ♦ K Q 10 7 4    W     E        ♦ 6 3
    ♣ A K             S            ♣ 9 6 5 4 2

                    ♠ A J 10 6 4
                    ♥ 10
                    ♦ A 8 5
                    ♣ Q J 8 3
```

Possible auction

South	West	North	East
—	—	Pass	Pass
1 ♠	1 NT	Pass	3 NT
Pass	Pass	Pass	

West has a difficult bid to find when South opens 1 S but an overcall
of 1 NT is clearly the best action. It indicates a strong, balanced type
of hand with a spade guard. East has no problem and simply responds 3 NT.

The ♠ 8 is led. Dummy plays low and South's ten forces the
queen. Declarer crosses to dummy with the ♥ A and leads a
diamond to the king. He then crosses to dummy with the ♥ K
intending to lead another diamond and play the queen unless South

contributes the ace. South duly obliges but not to trick five! He discards the ♦ A on trick four when dummy's ♥ K is played. This brilliant jettison play promotes his partner's ♦ J to a third round winner so that another spade can be led and four tricks cashed in that suit.

Declarer is doubly unlucky: once to find the hearts 6–1, and then to have an opponent clever enough to find such a brilliant discard.

TIP For defenders: unblock to create a vital entry in partner's hand.

BOARD 21   Dealer: North   North–South vulnerable   Room 1

```
                    ♠ 8 5
                    ♥ J 9 6 5 4 2
                    ♦ J 9 2
                    ♣ 10 7
    ♠ Q 9 3          N          ♠ K 7 2
    ♥ Q 7 3                      ♥ A K 8
    ♦ K Q 10 7 4   W     E       ♦ 6 3
    ♣ A K            S          ♣ 9 6 5 4 2
                    ♠ A J 10 6 4
                    ♥ 10
                    ♦ A 8 5
                    ♣ Q J 8 3
```

South	West	North	East
Martin Hoffman	Jeremy Flint	Rixi Markus	Irving Rose
—	—	Pass	Pass
1 ♠	1 NT	Pass	3 NT
Pass	Pass	Pass	

Good bidding, now for the play.

The ♥ 4 is led. What a setback! Surely Rixi Markus should have led a spade. Can it really be right to try to set up a six-card suit headed by the jack and with no outside entry? In this type of situation I have a very simple rule. I always lead my partner's bid suit. It may not always work, but it keeps partner happy.

Jeremy Flint wins in dummy and leads a diamond to the king, North playing the two. The ♥ 3 is led to the king and a diamond returned. Martin Hoffman plays the ♦ A and exits with the ♣ 3. Jeremy is under no pressure and soon makes ten tricks, scoring 430.

```
                         ♠ 8 5
                         ♥ J 9 6 5 4 2
                         ♦ J 9 2
                         ♣ 10 7
        ♠ Q 9 3              N          ♠ K 7 2
        ♥ Q 7 3                         ♥ A K 8
        ♦ K Q 10 7 4      W   E         ♦ 6 3
        ♣ A K                S          ♣ 9 6 5 4 2
                         ♠ A J 10 6 4
                         ♥ 10
                         ♦ A·8 5
                         ♣ Q J 8 3
```

South	West	North	East
Jane Priday	*Zia Mahmood*	*Omar Sharif*	*Rob Sheehan*
—	—	Pass	Pass
1 ♠	1 NT	Pass	3 NT
Pass	Pass	Pass	

Two consecutive bidding forecasts right!

The ♠ 8 is led and South's ten forces declarer's queen. Zia Mahmood is declarer and he quickly sees the point of the hand. He crosses to dummy with the ♥ A and leads a diamond playing the queen, North false cards with the nine. In my view this is a mistake; it is better to give partner a count by playing the two, showing three cards. South might then rise to the occasion subsequently by discarding the ♦ A.

Zia leads the ♥ Q. This is an excellent try. If Jane Priday jettisons the ♦ A, Zia intends to cash the ♦ Q, ♣ A K and the ♥ K before exiting with a club. This will be the end position:

```
                         ♠ —
                         ♥ J 6 5
                         ♦ J
                         ♣ —
        ♠ 9 3                N          ♠ K 7
        ♥ —                             ♥ —
        ♦ 10 7 4         W   E          ♦ —
        ♣ —                 S           ♣ 9 6 5
                         ♠ A J 6
                         ♥ —
                         ♦ —
                         ♣ Q J
```

Jane will win and although another club can be cashed, eventually dummy will make the ♠ K.

Instead of the play going this way, Jane counters by discarding the ♠ 4 on the ♥ Q! Zia cashes the ♣ A to 'muddy the waters' and then plays another heart to dummy's king. South slips from grace by discarding the ♣ 8. If instead the ♦ A is thrown declarer is defeated because he cannot prevent North from obtaining the lead with the ♦ J. Another spade lead would then be fatal.

The board was therefore flattened.

BOARD 22   Dealer: East   East–West vulnerable

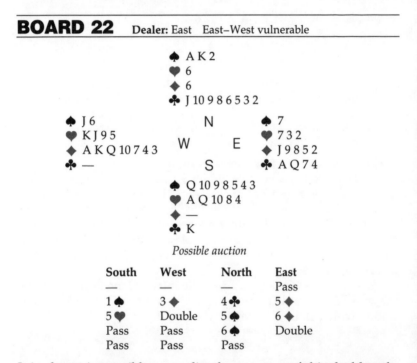

♠ A K 2
♥ 6
♦ 6
♣ J 10 9 8 6 5 3 2

♠ J 6
♥ K J 9 5
♦ A K Q 10 7 4 3
♣ —

♠ 7
♥ 7 3 2
♦ J 9 8 5 2
♣ A Q 7 4

♠ Q 10 9 8 5 4 3
♥ A Q 10 8 4
♦ —
♣ K

Possible auction

South	West	North	East
—	—	—	Pass
1♠	3♦	4♣	5♦
5♥	Double	5♠	6♦
Pass	Pass	6♠	Double
Pass	Pass	Pass	

It is almost impossible to predict the outcome of this deal but the side possessing the spade suit usually wins competitive auctions when the high cards are evenly split.

The ♦ A is led and ruffed by declarer. To come to twelve tricks declarer will have to establish clubs. Accordingly he leads the ♣ K at trick 2 and first West must refuse a cheap ruff and then East withhold his ♣ A. Although it is somewhat strange to duck declarer's only loser, it is essential. He might then have no losers, but he does not have twelve winners!

If the ♣K is taken by East, declarer can win the next trick and draw trumps ending in dummy. The ♣J is then led for a ruffing finesse and twelve tricks. Alternatively, if West ruffs, only one trump is required to draw trumps. Again the ♣J can be led for a ruffing finesse and subsequently the ♣10 will perform a similar function.

When the ♣K is allowed to win declarer is not quite beaten. He crosses to dummy with the ♠A and leads the ♣J. The correct defence, and again it may take an expert to see it, is for East to play the ♣7. Declarer is then really finished. If he ruffs high and crosses to dummy with the ♠A he cannot establish the clubs. If he discards a heart West ruffs and again declarer will fail to establish the clubs or ruff all his heart losers, and end up instead with eleven tricks.

TIP If entries are scarce, ducking by the defence can often kill a long suit in dummy.

BOARD 22 **Dealer:** East   East–West vulnerable   Room 1

```
                    ♠ A K 2
                    ♥ 6
                    ♦ 6
                    ♣ J 10 9 8 6 5 3 2
     ♠ J 6              N            ♠ 7
     ♥ K J 9 5                       ♥ 7 3 2
     ♦ A K Q 10 7 4 3   W   E        ♦ J 9 8 5 2
     ♣ —                  S          ♣ A Q 7 4
                    ♠ Q 10 9 8 5 4 3
                    ♥ Q 10 8 4
                    ♦ —
                    ♣ K
```

South	West	North	East
Martin Hoffman	*Jeremy Flint*	*Rixi Markus*	*Irving Rose*
—	—	—	Pass
1♠	Double	2♣	2♦
2♠	5♦	5♣	All pass

I was not enamoured with West's double, surely he would not have allowed his partner to play in hearts even if he had bid them. Top heavy hands do not usually play well in the shorter suit. Possibly there was a system difficulty. Perhaps 3 D would have been an American style weak jump overcall.

West leads the ♥5, obviously not too hopeful of his top diamonds cashing. Declarer, Martin Hoffman, wins with the eight and leads the ♣K. After some thought West correctly refuses to ruff and discards the ♦4. After further thought East plays the ♣A and leads the ♥7. Declarer wins, draws two rounds of trumps ending in dummy. He then claims his contract by taking the marked ruffing finesse in clubs. A heart ruff is his entry back to dummy.

I have stated in my preview that East should allow the ♣K to win. In defence of Irving Rose, he was not defending 6S, and his partner's initial heart lead made life very difficult. In fact twelve tricks cannot be prevented after this lead.

BOARD 22   Dealer: East   East–West vulnerable   Room 2

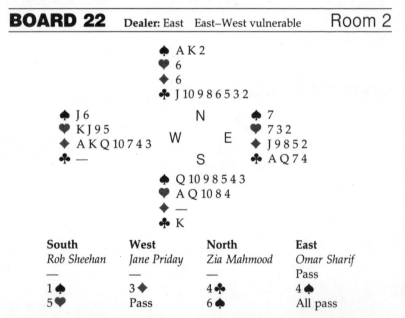

South	West	North	East
Rob Sheehan	Jane Priday	Zia Mahmood	Omar Sharif
—	—	—	Pass
1♠	3♦	4♣	4♠
5♥	Pass	6♠	All pass

Inadvertently this board was rotated ninety degrees clockwise so there were different team mates in Room 1 from Boards 21, 23 and 24.

The vulnerability factor probably prevented East–West from sacrificing; even with perfect defence of a heart lead and a ruff, West gets out for minus 800. Although, to be fair, East–West do have the balance of the high cards! Furthermore if they had found the best defence their action was justified.

An imaginative lead, the ♦3 is found by Jane Priday. Unfortunately for her, declarer ruffs her partner's jack. She reasoned that

Omar Sharif's 4♠ bid showed strong ♦ support.

With a different layout of the cards East could have won and by returning a club Jane could have defeated the contract by ruffing.

The ♣K is led and Jane passes her test by refusing to ruff. Unfortunately her partner fails his by winning with the ace! The ♠7 return is won in dummy and the other top trump honour played. Clubs are played until East wins and South ruffs. Declarer claims twelve tricks for a swing of 500 points (980 less 480 in Room 1).

BOARD 23   **Dealer:** South   Game all

```
                    ♠ 7 5 4 2
                    ♥ 9 2
                    ♦ A 9 4
                    ♣ K 7 6 2
  ♠ Q 10              N          ♠ A J 9 8
  ♥ K J 10 8 7 5 3              ♥ A Q 4
  ♦ K 7 5 2     W       E       ♦ 8 6 3
  ♣ —                 S          ♣ J 10 9
                    ♠ K 6 3
                    ♥ 6
                    ♦ Q J 10
                    ♣ A Q 8 5 4 3
```

Possible auction

South	West	North	East
1♣	1♥	2♣	3♣
Double	4♥	All pass	

The bidding sequence is interesting. West makes a simple overcall in hearts, his best action at this stage. It is most unlikely that he will not be given a second chance to describe his hand further. North supports his partner; it would be quite wrong to introduce his sparse spade suit. As it happens the raise to 2C embarrasses East who had intended to make that call himself as a cue bid to indicate a good raise to 2H. He has to improvise and decides to show a good raise to 3H instead. South doubles, indicating that he would have bid 3C himself but West has heard enough and goes to game. As it happens, 5C, even if doubled, is a cheap sacrifice (−200) but this is difficult to judge when the high cards are evenly divided.

The ♣2 is led which declarer ruffs. The contract, at first glance, seems to depend upon one of two finesses. The direct one in spades and the indirect finesse in diamonds. As can be seen, both are wrong and the contract may therefore seem to be doomed. A competent player would seek an additional chance, that of finding North with one of the club honours and a 2–1 trump break.

The sequence of play is to cross to dummy with the ♥ A and lead the ♣ 10. South must cover so declarer ruffs and re-enters dummy with the ♥ Q. Dummy's last club is led and this time, South cannot cover so declarer discards a spade. North wins and returns a spade which is won by dummy's ace. The planned position has arrived so declarer leads the ♠ J for a ruffing finesse. South covers and declarer ruffs. Dummy is entered by leading the ♥ 3 and overtaking with the ♥ 4. Two spade winners are then cashed and two losing diamonds discarded. Declarer then tries for an overtrick by leading a diamond to the king but he is unlucky and must settle for ten tricks. If he incautiously uses the ♥ 3 for ruffing or for entering dummy on the first or second round of trumps he will have to be content with nine tricks.

TIP Take care of the small cards and they will take care of you.

BOARD 23   Dealer: South   Game all   Room 1

```
              ♠ 7 5 4 2
              ♥ 9 2
              ♦ A 9 4
              ♣ K 7 6 2
  ♠ Q 10           N           ♠ A J 9 8
  ♥ K J 10 8 7 5 3             ♥ A Q 4
  ♦ K 7 5 2     W     E        ♦ 8 6 3
  ♣ —              S           ♣ J 10 9
              ♠ K 6 3
              ♥ 6
              ♦ Q J 10
              ♣ A Q 8 5 4 3
```

South	West	North	East
Martin Hoffman	*Jeremy Flint*	*Rixi Markus*	*Irving Rose*
1♣	3♥	4♣	4♥
5♣	Pass	Pass	Pass

Jeremy Flint's jump overcall of 3 H was interesting and deserved a better fate. A typical Rixi Markus bid of 4 C was North's riposte! 4 H by East and, inevitably, 5 C from South closed the auction.

Rixi's overbid of 4 C was extremely dangerous. As the partnership was using a strong no trump, Martin Hoffman could have had a three-card club suit and a weak no trump type of hand. It is doubtful, even if West passes, whether North should respond 1 S. That being so, 2 C is the only possible alternative. So you can judge how much of an overbid is 4 C.

There was nothing in the play of the hand. Declarer had three inescapable losers – a heart and two spades – and went one down, losing 100, even with both finesses right! We shall never know how Jeremy Flint would have played 4 H but credit must be given to Rixi for not giving him the chance.

BOARD 23   **Dealer:** South   Game all   Room 2

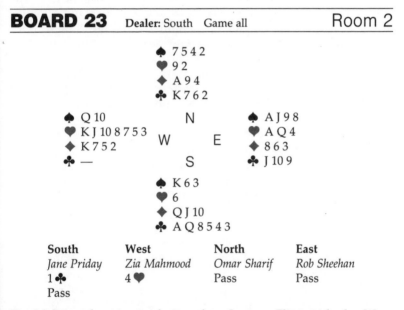

	North		
	♠ 7 5 4 2		
	♥ 9 2		
	♦ A 9 4		
	♣ K 7 6 2		

West: ♠ Q 10 ♥ K J 10 8 7 5 3 ♦ K 7 5 2 ♣ —

East: ♠ A J 9 8 ♥ A Q 4 ♦ 8 6 3 ♣ J 10 9

South: ♠ K 6 3 ♥ 6 ♦ Q J 10 ♣ A Q 8 5 4 3

South	West	North	East
Jane Priday	Zia Mahmood	Omar Sharif	Rob Sheehan
1 ♣	4 ♥	Pass	Pass
Pass			

Zia Mahmood goes one better than Jeremy Flint with the West hand. I wonder if even that bid would have silenced Rixi?

Omar Sharif thinks for a brief moment then places the ♠ 5 on the table! This is a killing lead and theoretically the contract cannot be made.

Zia, who in my opinion, was the unluckiest of all the participants, once again sees that he has been 'fixed'. It is just possible that Omar has made a true lead of his fourth best spade. By resorting to the Rule of Eleven (11–5, the pip value of the card led = 6), declarer knows that if this is so then South has no card higher than the five.

The reason is that he can see six higher cards in his own hand and dummy combined. Accordingly he finesses. South wins with the king and leads the ♦ Q so the defenders cash three diamond tricks for one down. Well led, Omar!

An alternative plan for Zia to have adopted would be based upon deception. He could play the ♠ A at trick one and follow with the queen from hand. The nonchalant play of the ♠ 8 might then catch South but I doubt if Jane Priday would have fallen for it, and so obviously did Zia because he did not attempt it.

There is a so-called 'kibitzer's make'. The ♠ A is played and then the ♣ 9 is led to trick two. South must cover with the ace or declarer discards a spade and allows North to win. The position is then similar to that described in the preview. Declarer ruffs the club with a high trump. Dummy is entered with the ♥ Q, declarer retaining the ♥ 3. The ♣ 10 is led and again South covers, this time with the queen. Declarer again ruffs high and re-enters dummy with the ♥ A. The ♣ J is then led on which declarer discards his losing spade. North wins and is endplayed. A spade return enables declarer to ruff South's king. He can then enter dummy by leading the ♥ 3 to the ♥ 4 and cash two winning spades for his contract. Another option for North is to lead a diamond but then declarer makes his king and ruffs a diamond in dummy for his tenth trick. The third possibility is to give a ruff discard.

Why 'kibitzer's make'? Well in this position Omar Sharif would undoubtedly choose to lead his fourth club giving a ruff discard. Why? Because it defeats the contract. Dummy can ruff and declarer discards a diamond but he still has three diamond losers.

Perhaps Rixi Markus should have chosen to defend in Room 1 after all. Assuredly so, if she were to lead a spade. Omar and his team mates on this board therefore scored 100 in both rooms.

BOARD 24   Dealer: West   Love all

```
              ♠ Q J 8 7 5
              ♥ A 8 6
              ♦ 3
              ♣ A J 3 2
♠ 10 9 6 2            N              ♠ A K 4 3
♥ —                                 ♥ K Q J 10 5 4 3
♦ A Q J 10 9 5 4 2  W   E           ♦ K 8
♣ 6                  S              ♣ —
              ♠ —
              ♥ 9 7 2
              ♦ 7 6
              ♣ K Q 10 9 8 7 5 4
```

Possible auction

South	West	North	East
—	4♦	Pass	6♦
7♣	Pass	Pass	Double
Pass	Pass	Pass	

Another bidding hand and again it is very difficult to predict the outcome. As the participants are not allowed to use the South African Texas Convention, West can afford the luxury of opening an old fashioned pre-emptive bid of 4 D. Although purists will dislike a pre-empt with a four-card spade suit in reserve, West can always pretend that the ♠ 2 was separated from the other spades and adjacent to his ♣ 6! A conventional bid of 4 D would indicate either a solid spade suit or a one loser spade suit with an outside ace. Similarly an opening bid of 4 C would have the same meaning but be based on a long heart suit. Supporters of the convention justifiably claim that its use ensures that the unknown hand remains concealed. This not only protects it from a possibly fatal lead but subsequently makes the defenders' task more difficult.

To return to the auction set out above, North is caught. He would like to bid but his values are tenuous. East, on the other hand, is delighted and makes the obvious call of 6 D. South is not going to be shut out, the opponents' bidding sounds too confident so he sacrifices in 7 C. Even with a blizzard opposite he should get out for 1100 and one trick from his partner will save 200 and the opponents may still make their small slam, worth 920.

West makes a forcing pass. He could double but he is not ashamed of his hand and by passing he informs his partner that he is not averse to playing in a grand slam if East has suitable controls. North also passes – he is wondering if the other three players are using the same pack of cards as he is! East has heard enough and double is the only sensible action. The ♦ A lead and a trump switch holds declarer to eleven tricks if he takes care to ruff his losing diamond and then ducks a low spade to West, discarding a heart. West is endplayed and must concede a ruff discard, or return a spade which is a vital entry for declarer to set up the long spade for another heart discard.

Should East–West persist in bidding 7 D, South will double to suggest that his partner finds an unusual lead, particularly not a club. North should realize that his partner is void in one suit and it must be in spades. He will be surprised to find that only this suit lead beats the contract and then by only one trick.

TIP Reassess your values in the light of a high level pre-emptive hand.

BOARD 24   **Dealer:** West   Love all   Room 1

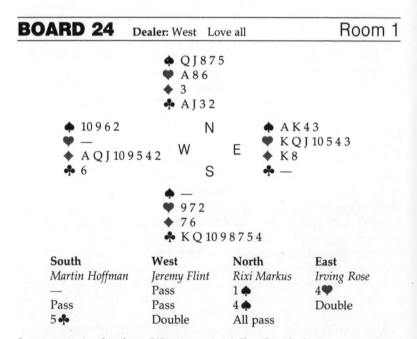

	♠ Q J 8 7 5	
	♥ A 8 6	
	♦ 3	
	♣ A J 3 2	

♠ 10 9 6 2	N	♠ A K 4 3
♥ —		♥ K Q J 10 5 4 3
♦ A Q J 10 9 5 4 2	W E	♦ K 8
♣ 6	S	♣ —

	♠ —	
	♥ 9 7 2	
	♦ 7 6	
	♣ K Q 10 9 8 7 5 4	

South	**West**	**North**	**East**
Martin Hoffman	*Jeremy Flint*	*Rixi Markus*	*Irving Rose*
—	Pass	1♠	4♥
Pass	Pass	4♠	Double
5♣	Double	All pass	

I was surprised to hear West pass initially. Good players sometimes employ this strategy because it may leave them better placed subsequently to judge whether or not to sacrifice. It has inherent dangers, however, when playing against Rixi Markus. After Rixi's opening bid of 1 S, Irving Rose decided that with a passing partner a slam was unlikely, so he simply called 4 H. When this came round to Rixi, she could easily have passed, as would at least 99.9% of the world's good players. She is, however, renowned for her so-called 'Rixi bids' and in this situation 4S came out like lightning. East doubled, and who would blame him. Martin Hoffman, sitting South, was not so happy and escaped to his eight-card suit. Jeremy Flint's double was uncharacteristic; I suspect he was worried that if he bid 5 ♦ it would show values in diamonds and heart tolerance – the auction went badly for him when Irving doubled 4 ♣. If Irving has heart length and at least three spades, it sounded like he was very short in diamonds. The ♦ A is led and the diamond continuation is ruffed. Martin led dummy's ♣ 5 but Irving did not fall from grace by splitting his honours. Instead he played the ♣ 4 so declarer ruffed. A low trump was then led and dummy's jack played. The ♠ 7 was led and when East contributed the three, Martin discarded the ♥ 2. West, no doubt still smarting at his fate, unluckily pulled the wrong card and dropped the ♠ 6 on the table. Declarer, therefore, ruffed a spade and soon claimed twelve tricks.

Martin's loser-on-loser play with the ♠ 7 was an example of good technique. From the bidding and initial lead he placed East with a seven-card heart suit, and Jeremy would certainly have led a heart if he had one. West therefore was void. By ducking the ♠ 7 to West he forced him either to return a spade, or to concede a ruff discard. Effectively this gave Martin an extra entry to dummy. Note that the ♣ 3 was too small to be used for that purpose.

This was the position:

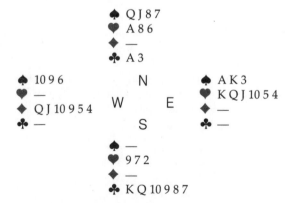

With the spades breaking 4–4 nothing could prevent Martin from making his contract. Jeremy's misfortune in pulling the wrong card did not therefore cost very much, merely an overtrick, 650 instead of 550.

BOARD 24   Dealer: West   Love all   Room 2

```
                    ♠ Q J 8 7 5
                    ♥ A 8 6
                    ♦ 3
                    ♣ A J 3 2
   ♠ 10 9 6 2              N              ♠ A K 4 3
   ♥ —                                    ♥ K Q J 10 5 4 3
   ♦ A Q J 10 9 5 4 2   W     E           ♦ K 8
   ♣ 6                      S              ♣ —
                    ♠ —
                    ♥ 9 7 2
                    ♦ 7 6
                    ♣ K Q 10 9 8 7 5 4
```

South	West	North	East
Jane Priday	*Zia Mahmood*	*Omar Sharif*	*Rob Sheehan*
—	5 ♦	Pass	6 ♦
Double	Pass	6 ♠	Double
7 ♣	Double	All pass	

On reflection I think that Zia Mahmood's bid of 5 D is the best action with the West hand. His partner's raise to 6 D was automatic and the only makeable slam contract easily reached. Jane Priday made a lightner slam double requesting North to make an unusual lead and if he had read it correctly he would obviously have chosen a spade because it was his longest suit and therefore the one in which his partner was most likely to be void.

When it was his turn to bid Omar Sharif had already decided that Rob Sheehan was employing a tactical manoeuvre of making an advance sacrifice on a worthless hand. In which case South had a very good hand, something like:

```
                    ♠ A K 10 9
                    ♥ K Q J 10
                    ♦ —
                    ♣ K Q 10 9 8
```

He was no doubt more concerned with missing a grand slam than the possibility of failing to make twelve tricks. Unfortunately for him the cards did not quite lie in the way he expected! Jane, of course, escaped to 7 C which Zia doubled.

Note, however, that Jane by doubling 6 D and Omar by bidding 6 S had saved their side from a bigger disaster, because 6 D is a make. After the initial lead of the ♠ Q South ruffs. If a trump is returned (best), West wins in dummy and ruffs a heart. A club ruff is followed by another heart ruff. Although the ♥ A does not fall, North is squeezed by the final trump. This is the ending:

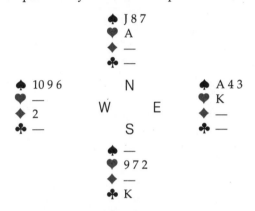

The ♦ 2 forces North to surrender.

Against Jane Priday's contract of 7 C doubled Zia Mahmood finds the excellent lead of the ♦ 2. This is the only lead to put his partner in so that he can return a heart for Zia to ruff. The ♦ 2 is chosen deliberately as a suit preference signal to request the return of the lower ranking of the two outside suits. Rob Sheehan wins the ♦ K and in turn makes a suit preference signal by leading the ♥ K to request a spade return. Zia wins and obliges but declarer is void in spades and ruffs. This results in declarer being able to set up the fifth spade for a heart discard and escape with losing two tricks, for a penalty of 300.

If Zia had played the ♦ A at trick three he would have achieved a 500 penalty because declarer does not have sufficient entries in dummy to set up the fifth spade because the ♣ 3 is worthless. Zia and his three team mates, however, will be well satisfied with their net 950.

It is time to change partners for the last round.

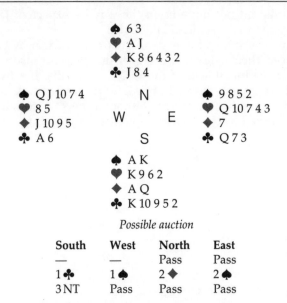

♠ 6 3
♥ A J
♦ K 8 6 4 3 2
♣ J 8 4

♠ Q J 10 7 4
♥ 8 5
♦ J 10 9 5
♣ A 6

♠ 9 8 5 2
♥ Q 10 7 4 3
♦ 7
♣ Q 7 3

♠ A K
♥ K 9 6 2
♦ A Q
♣ K 10 9 5 2

Possible auction

South	West	North	East
—	—	Pass	Pass
1♣	1♠	2♦	2♠
3 NT	Pass	Pass	Pass

North's bid of 2 D is questionable. It can only be justified because he has already passed and therefore partner is not forced to bid again. With his actual hand, however, South is happy to bid game.

The ♠ Q is led. Declarer wins and counts his tricks. If the diamonds break 3–2 there are ten on top but what if they are 4–1? The only chance then of setting up the suit is to finesse the ♥ J, hoping that West has the queen. The additional entry is required to establish the suit leaving the ♥ A in reserve as an entry to cash the two long diamonds. This looks reasonable but is there another chance? What about the club suit? If East has the ♣ Q it should be possible to make four tricks in that suit. Which is it to be? Echelon play provides the solution, declarer aims to combine the two chances.

The ♦ A is cashed and then the ♦ Q is led and overtaken by dummy's ♦ K. If the diamonds are 3–2 a diamond trick is conceded and declarer is home and dry. When East shows out on the second diamond, declarer is in the right hand to play clubs. He leads the ♣ 8 and finesses. West wins with the ace – it does not help to duck – and continues with another spade. Declarer wins, crosses to dummy with the ♥ A and repeats the club finesse by leading the jack and still makes ten tricks.

TIP When you have found a very good line of play look for a better one.

```
                        ♠ 6 3
                        ♥ A J
                        ♦ K 8 6 4 3 2
                        ♣ J 8 4
      ♠ Q J 10 7 4           N            ♠ 9 8 5 2
      ♥ 8 5                               ♥ Q 10 7 4 3
      ♦ J 10 9 5       W         E        ♦ 7
      ♣ A 6                               ♣ Q 7 3
                            S
                        ♠ A K
                        ♥ K 9 6 2
                        ♦ A Q
                        ♣ K 10 9 5 2
```

South	West	North	East
Jeremy Flint	*Jane Priday*	*Rixi Markus*	*Rob Sheehan*
—	—	Pass	Pass
1♣	1♠	2♦	2♠
3♥	Pass	4♣	Pass
4♦	Pass	Pass	Pass

This was a dreadful bidding sequence. South's bid of 3H, while academically accurate, was most unwise with an unfamiliar partner. North had already passed and surely therefore 3NT had to be the right action. North also should not have by-passed 3NT. A directional asking bid of 3S was essential. This is standard practice in expert circles and requests partner to bid 3NT if holding the spade suit guarded. Furthermore, North's hand improved as the auction progressed and if partner really had little in spades, all her cards were working. Despite the apparent minimum point count she had no right to pass 4D which was forcing to game once South had made a high level reverse. Note that it was still not too late to play in 4NT, which should be made.

There was nothing to the play, declarer merely lost a trump and a club trick, scoring 150.

```
                        ♠ 6 3
                        ♥ A J
                        ♦ K 8 6 4 3 2
                        ♣ J 8 4
   ♠ Q J 10 7 4            N            ♠ 9 8 5 2
   ♥ 8 5                                ♥ Q 10 7 4 3
   ♦ J 10 9 5       W          E        ♦ 7
   ♣ A 6                  S             ♣ Q 7 3
                        ♠ A K
                        ♥ K 9 6 2
                        ♦ A Q
                        ♣ K 10 9 5 2
```

South	West	North	East
Irving Rose	*Omar Sharif*	*Martin Hoffman*	*Zia Mahmood*
—	—	Pass	Pass
1 ♣	Pass	1 ♦	Pass
1 ♥	Pass	2 ♦	Pass
3 NT	Pass	Pass	Pass

I found it surprising that West did not overcall with 1 S. This gave North–South a free ride to find the best contract.

The ♠ Q is led. Irving Rose is declarer and he quickly sees that there are two lines of play, both very good. One line is to cash the ♦ AQ and then cross to dummy if they break 4–1 by finessing the ♥ J. This is to give an extra entry to set up the diamonds leaving the ♥ A as the card of access. The alternative line is to cash the ♦ A and overtake the ♦ Q with dummy's king. If the diamonds are 4–1 the suit is abandoned and declarer runs the ♣ J hoping that East has the queen.

Derek Rimington came to my rescue on this hand – I was feeling quite dizzy at the time trying to work out the odds – these are the findings of my knight in shining armour. Knowledge of percentage play determines which line should be followed.

There are three possible distributions of the diamond suit. These, with their relative percentage odds, are:

$$5–0 = 3.9\%$$
$$4–1 = 28.3\%$$
$$3–2 = 67.8\%$$

For practical purposes experts regard these percentages as 4, 28 and 68 respectively but in this example I will use the more accurate figures set out above.

The 67.8% is common to both lines of play and if the diamonds break 5–0 it will be necessary to find East with the ♣ Q so half of the 3.9% can be counted because the contract still succeeds. When the diamonds break 4–1 it is only West who can have the four cards when he follows to the ♦ A and the ♦ Q. It is therefore more likely that any particular card in the heart or club suits, in this case the queen of either, will be held by East in the proportion of 12–9. This is due to the theory of available places. The notional four diamonds take up four places in West's hand leaving nine. East has shown up with one diamond at the critical third trick and if this is a singleton he therefore had twelve available places for either of the key queens. Dividing 28.3 in the proportion of 12–9 gives 16.17 and 12.12 respectively. Irving's line of play was therefore superior to the alternative by 85.92% compared to 81.87%. Not a lot but enough to make the difference between winning or losing on this particular board.

I have set out the arithmetical calculations in detail to give the reader an insight of the way an expert's mind works. Many experts, however, do not bother to remember the accurate percentages involved but make do with the more common ones and then only with rough approximations. For example, as much of the two lines of play set out above is common to both, it is only necessary to know that the club finesse is 4–3 better than the heart finesse.

The swing on this board was worth 280 points.

BOARD 26 Dealer: East Game all

```
              ♠ K 10 4
              ♥ J 10 6 3
              ♦ A 10 9 7
              ♣ A Q
♠ A 8                        ♠ Q 5 2
♥ A 5            N           ♥ K Q 4
♦ 8 5 3 2      W   E         ♦ K Q 6 4
♣ K 10 8 4 3     S           ♣ J 9 6
              ♠ J 9 7 6 3
              ♥ 9 8 7 2
              ♦ J
              ♣ 7 5 2
```

Possible auction

South	West	North	East
—	—	—	1 NT
Pass	2 NT	All pass	

East has a near minimum opening bid and, unless playing the weak no trump, he would probably decide to pass. Yes, even thirteen points is not enough for a suit bid if the hand contains too many queens and jacks. West naturally raises to 2 NT but East correctly passes.

The ♣ 6 is led. During the bidding phase North should have started counting the high card points. East has shown at least twelve and West eleven. This leaves his partner with three at the very most. Accordingly when dummy's ♣ 8 is played at trick one, North cleverly follows with the ♣ 10. The only way to defeat the contract is for the defenders to take three spade tricks. The ♣ AQ and ♦ A are surely the only other tricks available. The snag about this plan is that the ♠ K wins trick one and the ♠ A wins trick two. If South has the ♠ Q all is well but he may have only jack to five in the suit and therefore never come to a spade trick. By playing the ♠ 10 North takes out some insurance. When he makes his ♣ Q he returns the ♠ K, sacrificed in a noble cause so that the lonely ♠ 4 becomes an entry card to South's established spade tricks.

TIP The Rule of Eleven in conjunction with your own holdings helps to defeat seemingly unassailable contracts.

```
                    ♠ K 10 4
                    ♥ J 10 6 3
                    ♦ A 10 9 7
                    ♣ A Q
    ♠ A 8              N            ♠ Q 5 2
    ♥ A 5                           ♥ K Q 4
    ♦ 8 5 3 2        W     E        ♦ K Q 6 4
    ♣ K 10 8 4 3       S            ♣ J 9 6
                    ♠ J 9 7 6 3
                    ♥ 9 8 7 2
                    ♦ J
                    ♣ 7 5 2
```

South	West	North	East
Jeremy Flint	*Jane Priday*	*Rixi Markus*	*Rob Sheehan*
—	—	—	1 NT
Pass	2 ♠	Pass	2 NT
Pass	Pass	Pass	

A very good bidding sequence. Rob Sheehan's 1 NT indicated 12–14 points. Jane Priday's 2 S bid was a transfer to clubs and when Rob denied having a good fit in clubs by bidding 2 NT instead of 3 C, Jane correctly passed. Generally the accepted requirements for rebidding the minor suit is three cards containing at least three points. Good players, however, usually treat an ace doubleton in the required minor suit as suitable.

The ♥ 9 is led. What a pity, a spade lead might have led to some attractive play. Rob wins in hand and runs the ♣ 9, Rixi Markus wins and switches to the ♦ 10. With her hand I would have thought a passive defence was necessary. Her partner can have nothing and therefore a heart trick should be established as soon as possible. Declarer wins, plays a heart to the ace and leads the ♣ 10. North wins and still gets busy by leading the ♠ 10. Declarer wins with the queen and eventually winds up with ten tricks for a score of 180.

```
                    ♠ K 10 4
                    ♥ J 10 6 3
                    ♦ A 10 9 7
                    ♣ A Q
    ♠ A 8              N            ♠ Q 5 2
    ♥ A 5                           ♥ K Q 4
    ♦ 8 5 3 2       W     E         ♦ K Q 6 4
    ♣ K 10 8 4 3       S            ♣ J 9 6
                    ♠ J 9 7 6 3
                    ♥ 9 8 7 2
                    ♦ J
                    ♣ 7 5 2
```

South	West	North	East
Irving Rose	*Omar Sharif*	*Martin Hoffman*	*Zia Mahmood*
—	—	—	1♦
Pass	2♣	Pass	2NT
Pass	3NT	All pass	

Unfortunately the bidding has got too high. Modern bidding theory is that when a strong no trump is being used, the sequence 1♦–2♣–2NT is not encouraging. West should therefore have passed with his eleven points, but it is not easy, because he also has a five-card club suit and the vulnerability is in his favour.

The ♠6 is led and Martin Hoffman plays the ten! There is no point in declarer ducking because Martin would then lead the ♠4 and set up a second spade trick. Zia Mahmood, who has quickly seen the point of the hand, therefore wins and finesses the ♣9 but it loses to the queen. Martin returns the ♠K. This very good defence by Martin achieves 200 when the contract goes two down for a swing of 380.

BOARD 27 Dealer: South Love all

```
                    ♠ 8 5 2
                    ♥ K 7 6
                    ♦ A 6 3
                    ♣ J 10 8 3
    ♠ J 10 3            N            ♠ A K
    ♥ A J 9                          ♥ Q 10 4
    ♦ J 10 9 7 4 2   W     E         ♦ K Q
    ♣ 5                 S            ♣ A K 7 6 4 2
                    ♠ Q 9 7 6 4
                    ♥ 8 5 3 2
                    ♦ 8 5
                    ♣ Q 9
```

Possible auction

South	West	North	East
Pass	Pass	Pass	2 ♣
Pass	2 ♦	Pass	3 ♣
Pass	3 ♦	Pass	3 NT
Pass	Pass	Pass	

East's hand is slightly too strong for an opening bid of 2 NT, the only possible alternative. When his partner responds with a negative 2 D, many experts would rebid 2 NT. On this hand it does not really matter, the final contract is bound to be 3 NT.

The ♠ 6 is led. Declarer wins and leads the ♦ KQ, North holding off. If the ♥ Q is finessed North wins and returns a spade establishing three spades for his partner. These, with his two tricks in the red suits, spell defeat.

The correct play is for declarer to lead the ♥ Q at trick four and play dummy's ♥ A. The ♦ J comes next and guess what? Declarer discards his spade winner. South cannot then run his spade tricks without allowing dummy to make a trick in the suit and that is the entry declarer needs to cash three diamond tricks. If the defenders refrain from leading spades, declarer wins the next trick and forces an entry to dummy by overtaking the ♥ 10.

Note that it is not good enough to play the ♥ 10 or ♥ 4 to dummy's ace at trick four. North will later prevent declarer from reaching dummy with a heart either by ducking the ♥ Q or by winning the ♥ J or ♥ 9.

TIP Create an entry by unblocking.

      ♠ 8 5 2
      ♥ K 7 6
      ♦ A 6 3
      ♣ J 10 8 3

♠ J 10 3   **N**   ♠ A K
♥ A J 9   ♥ Q 10 4
♦ J 10 9 7 4 2   **W**   **E**   ♦ K Q
♣ 5   **S**   ♣ A K 7 6 4 2

      ♠ Q 9 7 6 4
      ♥ 8 5 3 2
      ♦ 8 5
      ♣ Q 9

South	West	North	East
Jeremy Flint	*Jane Priday*	*Rixi Markus*	*Rob Sheehan*
Pass	Pass	Pass	2 NT
Pass	3 NT	All pass	

I have no quarrel with this bidding sequence. An opening bid of
2 NT with the East hand is eminently practical. Jane Priday's response of 3 NT is just the action expected of a good player. There is
no point in bidding diamonds; a slam is most unlikely and the
singleton club is certain to be adequately covered by East.

The ♣ 6 is led. Rob Sheehan inspects dummy and rises to the
occasion by playing exactly as I had forecast in the preview. He wins
the ♠ K and cashes the ♦ KQ, North correctly holding off. The
♥ Q comes next and the ace is played. The ♦ J is led and the ♠ A
discarded. The lead of the ♣ J is won and the ♥ 4 led to dummy's
nine. North wins with the king and leads another club. Rob wins
with the king and crosses to dummy with the ♥ J in order to run the
established diamonds for ten tricks.

Sammy Kehela and I immediately make an entry in our notebooks
about this play. It must be one to be seriously considered when we
meet to discuss the winner of the Brilliancy Prize.

```
                    ♠ 8 5 2
                    ♥ K 7 6
                    ♦ A 6 3
                    ♣ J 10 8 3
    ♠ J 10 3            N            ♠ A K
    ♥ A J 9                          ♥ Q 10 4
    ♦ J 10 9 7 4 2   W     E         ♦ K Q
    ♣ 5                 S            ♣ A K 7 6 4 2
                    ♠ Q 9 7 6 4
                    ♥ 8 5 3 2
                    ♦ 8 5
                    ♣ Q 9
```

South	West	North	East
Irving Rose	*Omar Sharif*	*Martin Hoffman*	*Zia Mahmood*
Pass	Pass	Pass	2♣
Pass	2♥	Pass	2NT
Pass	4♦	Pass	4♥
Pass	4NT	Pass	5♥
Pass	6NT	All pass	

Another wheel come off. West obviously thought that the partnership were playing the CAB System (Club, Aces and Blackwood).

A feature of the CAB system is that responder shows his aces in
response to an opening bid of 2 C. 2 D is a denial but 2 H, 2 S, 3 C and
3 D indicate the ace of the bid suit. 3 NT indicates any two aces, and
2 NT shows an aceless hand with at least eight points containing
two or more kings. 3 H, 3 S, 4 C and 4 D responses show a solid suit
without the ace. Please don't feel I am encouraging anyone to take
up this system!

In the bidding shown 2 NT and 4 D were intended as natural but
4 H was to play, assuming partner had a good red two-suiter, and
5 H showed two aces. 4 NT may have been meant as quantitative but
the waters were really too muddied by then.

The ♠ 4, an attitude lead, is made. In this convention a low card
lead is encouraging, promising an honour in the suit, and a medium
size card, discouraging. Zia Mahmood, the declarer, wins and is in
a hopeless position. He plays the ♦ KQ which are allowed to win.
The ♥ 4 is led and the nine finessed. North wins and seeing that he
has won the board, incorrectly cashes the ♦ A. I know that it is very
late but did he really think that the ♦ A was going to run away?

A spade return would have put the contract four down. A score of 50, plus the 430 earned by Rob Sheehan in the other room, nevertheless still makes a handsome result.

BOARD 28   **Dealer:** West   North–South vulnerable

```
              ♠ J 9 7 5 2
              ♥ 9 7 5
              ♦ 8 7 4
              ♣ 8 4
  ♠ K Q 10         N          ♠ 8 4
  ♥ Q J 6 3                   ♥ A 2
  ♦ A 6 5 2     W     E       ♦ Q 3
  ♣ J 2             S          ♣ K Q 10 9 7 5 3
              ♠ A 6 3
              ♥ K 10 8 4
              ♦ K J 10 9
              ♣ A 6
```

Possible auction

South	West	North	East
—	1 NT	Pass	3 NT
Pass	Pass	Pass	

When East hears his partner open a weak no trump he realizes that there is no point in bidding his club suit. The hand must play better in a nine-trick contract than one where eleven tricks are required.

North leads the ♠ 5 to South's ace. When West follows with the ♠ 10 South can accurately place almost every high card. Furthermore, he should see that he can kill dummy's club suit if West has only a doubleton club. At trick two he therefore returns the ♥ K which forces dummy's ace. When clubs are played the ♣ A is held up and dummy is about ready to be consigned to the waste paper basket. The vain hope of a low diamond to the queen for an indirect finesse may be attempted but to no avail.

West, however, has a counter to this entry destroying play which is known as the Merrimac Coup. It is to play the ♥ 6 on South's ♥ K and dummy's ace. Subsequently when he wins the ♠ K or the ♥ Q he can cash all his winning cards outside diamonds and then exit with the ♥ 3! South is helpless and is forced to take the trick and lead back a diamond, away from his king. Declarer thus makes ten tricks, losing the two black aces and the ♥ 4. Bridge, at times, is a funny game. Sammy Kehela and I decided that if either of the two Wests played the ♥ 6 on the ♥ K we would have no hesitation in awarding the Brilliancy Prize.

TIP For defenders: when dummy has a long broken suit and is short of entries, attack the entry if your own hand tells you that by returning your partner's lead you cannot defeat the contract.

BOARD 28   Dealer: West   North–South vulnerable   Room 1

```
                    ♠ J 9 7 5 2
                    ♥ 9 7 5
                    ♦ 8 7 4
                    ♣ 8 4
    ♠ K Q 10              N              ♠ 8 4
    ♥ Q J 6 3                            ♥ A 2
    ♦ A 6 5 2      W         E           ♦ Q 3
    ♣ J 2                                ♣ K Q 10 9 7 5 3
                         S
                    ♠ A 6 3
                    ♥ K 10 8 4
                    ♦ K J 10 9
                    ♣ A 6
```

South	West	North	East
Jeremy Flint	*Jane Priday*	*Rixi Markus*	*Rob Sheehan*
—	1 NT	Pass	3 NT
Pass	Pass	Pass	

The last board and the participants have been in the studio playing on and off for nearly sixteen hours. No wonder that the strain has been showing.

The bidding sequence was accurate. Rob Sheehan realizes that there is no point in showing his club suit. The best chance of game must be no trumps so he simply bids it.

The ♠ 5 is led and Jeremy Flint wins with the ♠ A and returns the ♥ K. This, as I have already stated, is the Merrimac Coup, an entry destroying play where an unsupported honour is deliberately sacrificed. The coup is aptly named after the *Merrimac*, an American collier which was sunk in 1898 in Santiago harbour in an attempt to bottle up the Spanish fleet.

Declarer is upset by this manoeuvre and too hurriedly follows suit with the ♥ 3. Jeremy ducks the first club but wins the second and exits with a spade. Declarer tries to throw Jeremy in by cashing the ♥QJ and the ♠Q before leading the ♥6 but Jeremy carefully keeps unblocking, retaining the ♥4 to play on the ♥6 and defeat the contract by one trick.

BOARD 28   Dealer: West   North–South vulnerable   Room 2

```
                    ♠ J 9 7 5 2
                    ♥ 9 7 5
                    ♦ 8 7 4
                    ♣ 8 4
    ♠ K Q 10              N            ♠ 8 4
    ♥ Q J 6 3                          ♥ A 2
    ♦ A 6 5 2      W         E         ♦ Q 3
    ♣ J 2                              ♣ K Q 10 9 7 5 3
                         S
                    ♠ A 6 3
                    ♥ K 10 8 4
                    ♦ K J 10 9
                    ♣ A 6
```

South	West	North	East
Irving Rose	Omar Sharif	Martin Hoffman	Zia Mahmood
—	1 ♥	—	2 ♣
Pass	2 NT	Pass	3 NT
Pass	Pass	Pass	

A variation in the bidding sequence no doubt necessitated because the partnership have agreed to use the strong no trump. The final contract was still a good one.

The ♠5 is led. Irving Rose, South, wins the ♠A and like his counterpart, Jeremy Flint in Room 1, returns the ♥K. Declarer also makes the mistake of parting with the ♥3 and play develops in precisely the same way as before. The result too, is similar and we therefore end the tournament with a tied board.

The Winner

In an individual tournament of this type it is very difficult to determine the best player. The reason is simply that one may play very well but be let down by one's partners. Also with prepared hands some are more difficult than others.

In a Par contest, along the lines of the World Championships of 1961 and 1963, this is recognized by the composers awarding points for bidding sequences which reach the best contract. The composers' bidding sequence, hence the final contract and declarer, is also stated and points are awarded if the initial leader selects the correct card. Points are also awarded for play and defence. In this manner a fair contest can be organized for competing pairs with separate North–South and East–West winners.

Time and technical reasons, however, prevented this tournament being organized as a Par contest, and it was also considered preferable to have eight participants competing as individuals. The winner could have been determined by simple aggregate scoring, with or without honours counting. Another possible method was to use international match point scoring as is used in World Teams Championships. A third possibility was point-a-board scoring which is very popular in some teams tournaments in the USA. This could have been supplemented by the use of a graded aggregate scale (6–0, 5–1, 4–2, and 3–3 for example).

Whichever method is used it is impossible to find the same participant emerging as the outright winner. Principally, for this reason the Channel Four television producer David Elstein decided in advance that a Brilliancy Prize would be awarded to the player of the series. Sammy Kehela, the Canadian World Master, who has assisted me with the commentary on the programme, was appointed as one of the judges. I was the other. Here are our findings.

All the participants attained a high standard on particular boards. For all round excellence and particularly the spectacular play as declarer in a contract of 3 NT on Board 20, in the early hours of the morning, we consider that Rob Sheehan was outstanding. Accordingly we awarded him the Channel Four Brilliancy Prize.

This book was published during the television series: sadly for the reader, it would have been unfair to television viewers to give the game away before its end by revealing the name of the winner – the player who does best with all partners.